Visualizing Social Interactions
A Guide to Effective Communications

Michael J. Pritchard

Book Design & Illustrations: Michael J. Pritchard
Cover Design: Michael J. Pritchard
Edited By: Douglas J. Pritchard
Photography By: Heidi A. Pritchard

PO Box 442032
Lawrence, KS 66044

Date: 4/15/2011
ISBN: 1456327089
ISBN-13: 978-1456327088

To Heidi, Sydney and Zander

Table of Contents (Chapter 1 – 7)

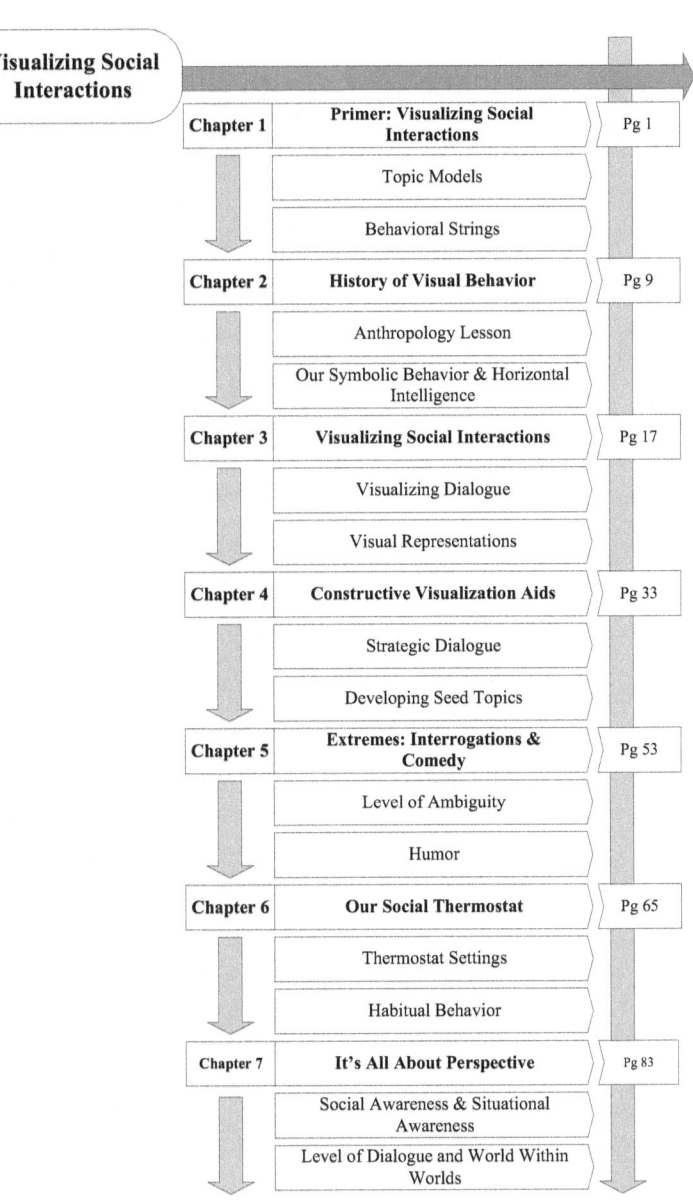

Table of Contents (Chapter 8 – 9)

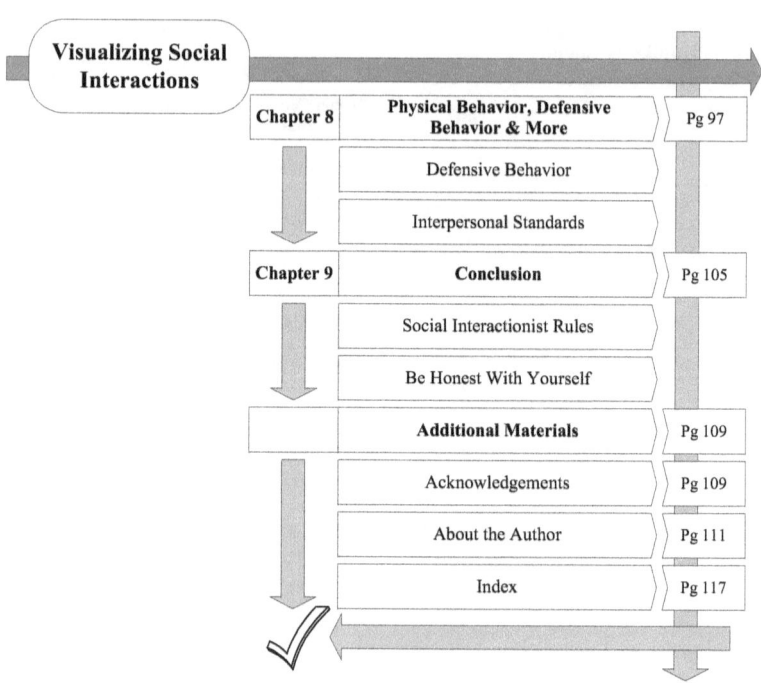

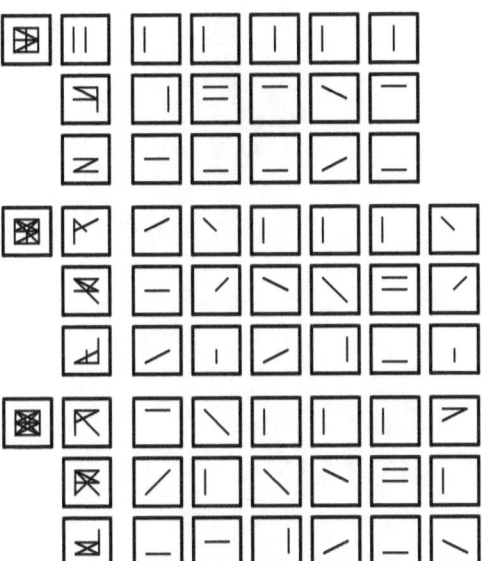

Purpose

For professional or personal, this book is intended for people interested in visually deconstructing social situations. We are going to investigate visual methods that help shape our thought processes so that we may better respond to the world around us. We will also investigate how we can visually manage our surrounding environment…not necessarily to control, but so that we are better equipped to shape and navigate the complex world we live in.

We are smart people. We have a great deal of knowledge that we have cultivated over our lifetimes. As a hyper-specialized society, the deck is stacked against us when it comes to exchanging information. When we engage in dialogue with others we tend to shift our conversations towards our own comfort zones. This is understandable as our own communication style is filled with specialized facts about our own piece of the world. It is a language and culture that few understand. Regrettably this acquired knowledge can also be our greatest liability. The unfortunate reality is that our knowledge base is literally of interest to one person…our self…the "Country of Me".

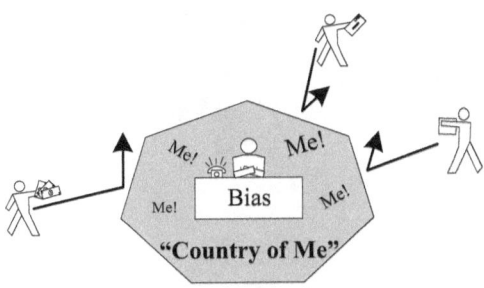

We want to reshape our behavior such that we are not closed off to the world around us. This involves reassessing what we think we understand about ourselves. This means that we have to be comfortable with seeking out and exposing ourselves to the variety of life.

From behavioral analysis to visualizing social interactions, we want to augment our built in ability to relay information to others in a more deliberate and measured manner. The road is not easy. At the heart of each and every one of us is an animal. It takes determination and persistence to recondition our behavior so that we may influence our inner animal. Sticking to this process can yield new insights into not only our internal thought processes; it can also help to better inform our perspective, placement and purpose.

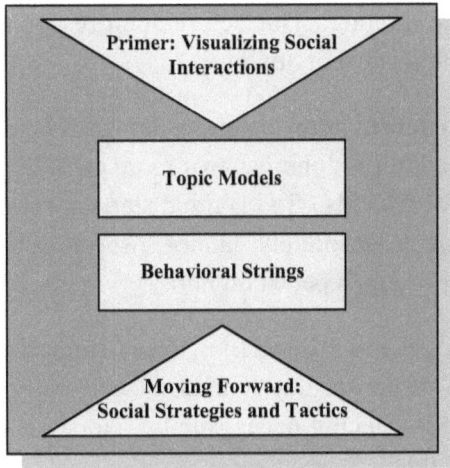

Chapter One – Visualizing Interactions, a Primer...

John is a machinist. He makes aluminum parts for a local manufacturing company. John and his wife have two children, a three bedroom house, two cars, a boat and motorcycle. He made a run at college, but put those plans on hold after the second baby. John works a regular shift, but lately work has started to slow. One day John gets called in to see the boss:

> John's Boss – "John, business has started to slow down. When I worked in your shoes many years ago I was able to machine ten parts an hour. Now I see that the production on your line has decreased to 7 parts per hour. What is the deal?"

The statement freezes John in his tracks. John wants to respond to his boss, but he is unsure of how he should approach the situation. John understands that business is slow due to outside economic pressures that have translated to a decrease in demand for his machined parts. Since the market is getting a little sluggish John is left wondering what is the REAL intent behind this line of questioning. But before John responds to his boss, he gets hit with a wave of anxiety.

John bought a new motorcycle and a new bass boat and put it all on credit. In addition, John has two more car bills, medical bills and daycare for the kids. So his mind starts to race. John thinks to himself that he absolutely cannot lose the job. Financially speaking, everything depends on him.

John starts to get more butterflies in his stomach. His boss is waiting for a response, but John does not really have a good answer. John is dancing on eggshells. He starts to respond as calmly as possible:

> John – "…boss…ummm…you know…well…"

John starts to think to himself that he cannot call his boss out on the tough economic conditions. He cannot control his shaky voice. John is really nervous about drawing this process out. He just wants it to be over. Again, his thoughts quickly become preoccupied with finances. He has fully leveraged his income and he literally has nothing left in the bank at the end of each paycheck. It would be disastrous if he ends up without a job to an already strained situation. The psychological assault of a simple question has run its course. John can no longer think clearly and he finally responds:

> John – "…Boss, I guess I see your point…I will try harder…"

John leaves the office and wonders about the conversation that just took place. Should he have said more? He also contemplates ulterior motives. John knows that his boss is fully aware of the current economic conditions. Yet, John begins to see another picture forming. John's affirmation of his boss's conclusion could easily be taken to indicate that John is taking the blame. In his mind, it was a simple performance issue. John is upset that he never really clarified with his boss where the direction of the conversation was going. John starts to think with more clarity that maybe his boss was looking for other factors. But now he realizes that he took the blame for something that was out of his control. John starts to realize that he was socially outgunned.

Resolving John's Dilemma…

Let us break down John's Dilemma to see what is going on visually. We do this in two steps. First we do some topic modeling. We want to get the high-level items captured. Next, we need to do some behavioral sequencing[1] to get a handle on how all the contributing pieces are influencing John's present state of affairs. A visual representation of John's situation should be simple yet broad:

John's Life

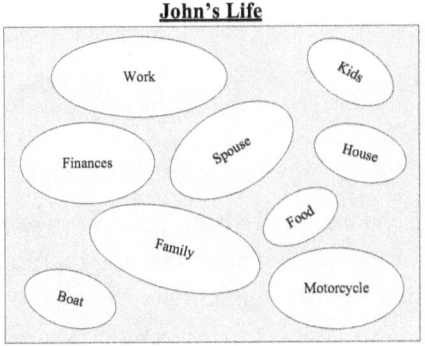

---

[1] When we say "Behavioral Sequencing" we are referring to the chain of events that occur in our behavior. In other words, our socially constructed framework takes on a series of linear steps. Sequencing this behavior is key in understanding where disconnects occur. Think of it as our "daily" work flow, but from a social perspective.

Now that we have John's behavior grouped we can begin to sequence the situation. First, it is critically important that John's behavior be approached with a strong sense of reality. A lack of honesty will only perpetuate the existing social dynamics that we are trying to resolve for John. Second, we need to determine how his social interactions are influencing each other. We do this by creating a behavioral string diagram:

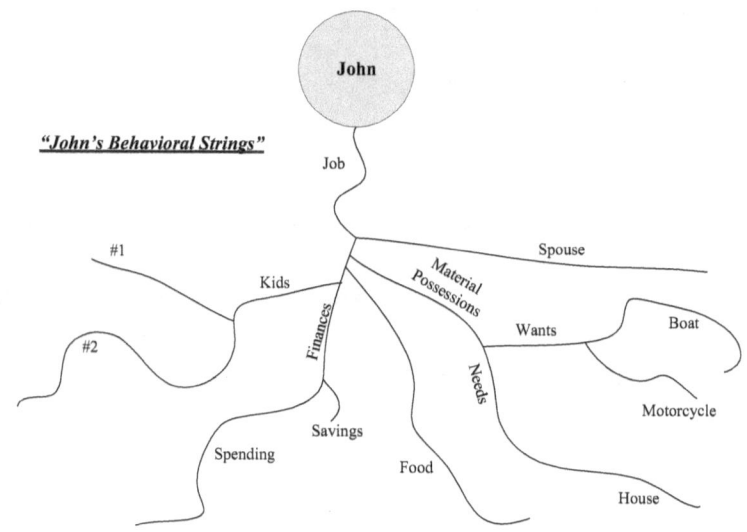

When drawing a behavioral string diagram, we need to keep a couple rules in mind. The length of a line represents the amount that is socially invested in that activity. For example a short line equals a short investment. The investment is a relationship. The relationship can be anything like social activities, personal relationships or financial responsibilities.

1) A behavioral analysis needs to include an honest assessment of "needs versus wants". This can come from a materialistic and/or a social perspective.

2) Be on the lookout for excessive dependencies and relationship entanglements ("social knotting").

After carefully reviewing John's situation we can begin to get an idea of where the "knotting" is occurring in John's life. Basically, we can see that the bottleneck in his life is that everything is wrapped up in his job. John has essentially created a series of dependent behavioral strings that all converge on his job. John made recent loans to purchase a motorcycle and boat. As illustrated on the diagram, he has very little in terms of savings. He does not have a backup plan or any contingency skills to leverage. Financially he is 100% leveraged; there is nothing that is not entangled with John's job. John's financial situation has permeated his personal life as well.

John's Post-Meeting Analysis (Hot Wash)

After reviewing his situation, John decides that he needs to make some tough decisions. He has to be honest about the boat, motorcycle, spending and savings. He also needs to add in some new behavior that helps to shield him from job loss, so new training or college maybe required to help protect John's family from losing everything.

John starts to see that he needs to untangle the "knotted behavior". So he goes about creating a future state for himself, a vision of what he would like to see down the road.

John takes a hard look at his situation; he decides that he needs to sell the boat and motorcycle to create a little financial breathing room. This also has the added benefit of creating more cash that can be used for savings. But John also realizes the precarious nature of the job, so he decides that training at the local community college as a paramedic is an excellent contingency track. He certainly needs to get "buy in" from his family and talks it over openly with all family members.

Fast forwarding a few years John's adjusted behavior looks like this:

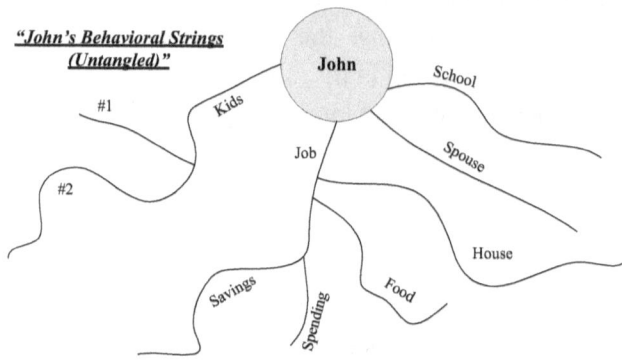

John's behavioral strings have become greatly simplified. His job is no longer creating dependencies upon all factors of his life. John "clipped" the motorcycle and boat strings. This subsequently drove up his savings ability. While his family still requires the job, his wife and kids are no longer DIRECTLY tied to his prior financial habits. Lastly, John has created contingency behavior by pursuing another line of work through schooling. This has built up his confidence at his current job allowing him to talk with greater confidence.

Conclusion…

We all have our own unique story to tell, and our dependencies will all be different. We will talk about "behavioral strings" in more detail (Chapter 6, Social Thermostat). These situations have to be viewed from a positive "big picture" perspective. We have to tackle these situations in a strategic way so that we can tactically carry out our goals. While we often understand the dependencies between our job, finances and family we often times underestimate the seriousness of our own dilemmas. We forget about the other dependencies that are contributing factors to the total anxiety that is being introduced into the whole situation (i.e. a thousand dollar dress, or power tool, is really only eighty dollars a month on credit!). We get a better handle on what to attack by strategically visualizing our social interactions. It puts it on paper, and imprints that object in our memory in a more lasting way.

We all live complex lives. The last thing we need is an overly academic lecture on all the tiny little nuisances of communication. This book is not meant to be academic. This book is intended to stimulate our internal dialogue and curiosity. There is so much information that is available to us. To that end, the many topics contained within this book are labeled with footnotes and keyword searches. These keyword searches have been intentionally created to put the power of curiosity in our hands. We need to consider the world around us. We need to explore our surroundings, diagnose the issues, introduce therapies and evaluate their outcomes so that we can grow as an individual.

If we have ever asked ourselves the following:

- How can we better organize our social activities?
- What tools do we need to cultivate our personal relationships?
- How do we enhance our professional and personal interactions?
- How do we maintain our composure in tough situations?

- How do we develop and successfully execute our life goals?
- What perspectives and attitudes are required for success?

….then the tips, trick, tools and lessons learned in this book will increase our ability to visualize and realize our life pursuits.

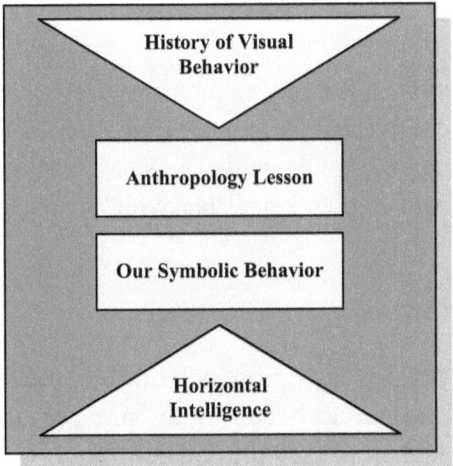

Chapter Two – A History of Our Visual Behavior...

It is important to understand some of the basics when it comes to our visual and symbolic behavior. Our prehistoric lineage really has a lot to do with how visual we are as a species. For starters, let us take a peek at the last 200,000 years over a speedy three pages.

The most conclusive research to date shows that modern symbolic behavior occurred 167,000 years ago at Pinnacle Point[2]. Evidence has suggested that humans began to create paint and began regular harvesting of marine resources. Moving from Southern Africa and up to Northern Africa we see more evidence of modern behavior documented in the Atlas Mountains (modern day Sahara) at around 82,000 years ago. This time period is rather important because it is recognized as

---

[2] Keyword Internet Search: "Symbolic Behavior" + "Pinnacle Point"

the first point in time where arrow point technology[3] was introduced.

While the advancement of weapons was well on its way, other areas had also advanced. Evidence of seasonal migration, cave paintings, micro-economic trade, bone carvings and ritualistic burial all help to define a new behavior[4] that was not seen in previous generations.

The Advancement of Symbolic Thought.....

Moving into modern day France, starting at around 40,000 years ago[5] we begin to see art occurring in more complex forms. At Chauvet Cave, charcoal samples taken from 2 rhinoceros and 1 bison were dated to roughly 31,000 years ago. From 42,000 years ago to 10,000 years ago these cultural industries developed a large majority of all the art we will see up to this point. The variety of prehistoric art becomes amazingly complex and extensive. The case for symbolic behavior is unequivocal during this time period.

Value of Symbolic Behavior...

There are many theories from many different disciplines that offer insight into our own visually stimulated behavior. From the preservation perspective, this behavior allows us to store a concept and transmit that concept over time. In other words, our thoughts can be carved in stone or written on paper, allowing us to visually communicate long after a culture has passed. From an educational perspective, a large concept can be broken down into a smaller concept, so as to make it more understandable.

---

[3] Keyword Internet Search: "Aterian Industry" + "Middle Stone Age"
[4] Keyword Internet Search: "Aurignacian Culture" or "Gravettian Culture"
[5] Keyword Internet Search: "Chauvet Cave Paintings"

From a hunting perspective, advantages are granted to those able to stay silent while remaining in communication (i.e. a hunting party). Lastly, our symbolic behavior allows us to visualize and imagine a conceptual world not bound by physical properties.

Although most mammals apply a "vertical intelligence" to their surroundings, humans take a different approach. Humans can associate multiple different "knowledge bases", creating a kind of "horizontal intelligence" across domains. This allows for the integration of multiple subjects. For example, a typical predator might look at prey in a limited number of verticalities: food type and time of day. However, humans may integrate many multiple verticalities when hunting: food type, tool type, time of day, time of year, weather, and terrain. Humans are more "situationally aware" because they can cross compare different knowledge domains. Our unique behavior bridges the gap between different knowledge bases by aggregating subjects into one coherent thought.

Historical Recap…

As social creatures we instinctually understand the social dynamics that form both individual and group communications. Our prehistoric ancestors have evidenced this on cave paintings, wall art, stone work and figurines[6]. This phenomenon is interesting in that it tells us that so much of our origins are based on a "visual cueing" system. When humans rediscovered art work at Lascaux Cave in France[7], we found visual representations of the world around us, or more specifically the visual representations of how humans viewed their world at that given point in time.

---

[6] Hohlenstein-Stadel "Lion Man" was carved nearly 32,000 years ago in what anthropologist classify as the Aurignacian cultural period.

[7] Lascaux Cave in southwest France has cave paintings that are estimated to be over 17,000 years old.

Human expansion from small tribes into larger chiefdoms led to an increasing need to categorize concepts. Agriculture, warfare, astronomy and cultural expansion in general helped to spur the need for a complex symbolic representation of our thought processes. We in turn developed writing systems that allowed us to harden ideas and concepts.

Moving into modern times, humans have evolved ever increasing ways to store and categorize human thoughts. With computer storage systems on the rise, we are now able to store more information than we can conceivably process. In a way, we are going through a kind of "information overload". Our capacity to store information is far outreaching our ability to analyze that information. We now find ourselves saddled with too much information making it nearly impossible to make a decision about anything. When we go out for something as simple as groceries our mind has to mentally "table scan" our knowledge base, or we pull out our touch phone, to determine which food store best approximates what we are trying to achieve on this particular grocery run....it is downright awful. We are in a state of "cerebral paralysis".

Due to the immense amount of information available to us, we have created special interpreters for each specialization. As a society, we have become so technically specialized that we have doctors, lawyers, electricians, mechanics, accountants, teachers, business planners, project managers, and the list goes on and on. In the end we are all specialists. We all have our own special area of interest. And we need to explore ways to cut through the information clutter so that we can more effectively interrelate to each other. In so doing, we have to become comfortable with learning all over again.

Sally's Story: Starting Fresh…

After graduating from high school Sally was done. Going back to school was not for her. So she had started a side business and figured that would be good enough for the time being. Over the years, Sally picked up specialized trade skills, but the economy was tough. She decided that additional training was required. So after much deliberation she decided to give college a go and enrolled at a local community college.

Sally had to take a placement exam before she could enroll in any college courses. She was a decent student in high school and felt more than prepared for the upcoming exam.

After taking the exam, Sally was in for a rude awakening. She had to take remedial math and remedial English before she could enroll in any kind of freshman level college courses. In other words, Sally was not even a college freshman! She was literally back to the basics. Without a doubt she was frustrated. Her prospects for getting additional training were looking pretty slim.

Sally wrestled with this for a couple weeks and she slowly began to look at it from a different perspective. After talking to friends and family, and being brutally honest with herself, it became clear that it would be good for her to start fresh. Sally began to look at it less as a failure on her part and more of an opportunity to restock and to reboot. Sally turned her perspective upside down. The negative was replaced with a positive.

A Review of Sally's Situation…

In looking back on Sally's situation, two important points jump out. First, we have to understand that we do not know as much as we think we know. Second, it is okay to not know everything. Our acquired knowledge is both an asset and a liability. In this case, our knowledge base creates bias in our thinking.

To learn how to visualize social interactions, we must learn to get rid of our "biases". We are human, and therefore incapable of perfection. But to the best of our abilities we have to remove "biases" from our thought process when approaching social situations. We must strive to unlearn our past so that we can fill ourselves up with fresh new information. This means that our imprinted philosophies of religion, business, politics, family history, work history, etc...all have to be cleared out of the attic and to a certain extent re-examined. This does not mean we have to abandon our ideologies. However, we have to give our minds room to breathe and expand. We need to create space to grow...and unfortunately our biases take up A LOT of room.

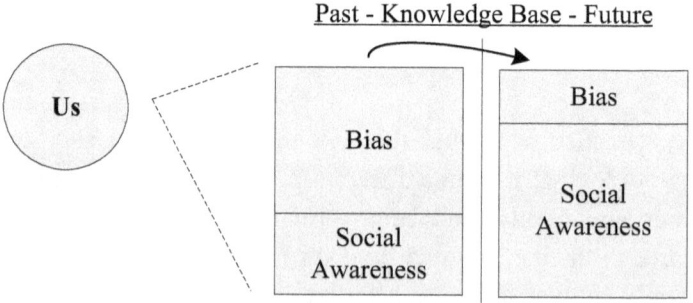

Past - Knowledge Base - Future

Conclusion...

We want to expand our knowledge base beyond our ingrained biases that we grew up with. This means that we need to bombard ourselves with variety. While it is great to have our favorites, we need to dabble with other entrees in the "menu of life". The more variety we introduce in our lives the more socially aware we become.   If we are focused on being a "Country of Me", then we limit our ability to experience what life has to offer.   Our goal is to take in what we learn through this process to help maximize on this concept…not only for our social awareness, but our professional and cultural awareness as well.

New Experiences

Learn Something Exotic
Do Something Completely New
Be Different and Bold
Volunteer Your Expertise
Develop A New Skill

Social Interactions

Maintain Positive Attitude
Remove My Biases
Keep an Open Mind
Have a Longitudinal Perspective
Learn to Be Collaborative

Personal Relationships

Set Boundaries
Develop a Good Personal Network
Develop Positive Family Relationships
Be Yourself, Not Others

Travel Experiences

Backpack Across Europe
Spend a Week in Thailand
Hiking in the Ozarks

Educational Experiences

Read, Read and Read
Enroll In That Class
Get Vetted By An Authority
Develop Self Reflective Honesty

Professional Goals

Be The Knowledge Authority
Help Out with an Oil Change
Speak at a Group Meeting
Author an Article
Put Yourself Into New Situations

Personal Ambitions

Get A Degree
Get A Pilot's License
Make Your Spouse Laugh
Make Your Kids Laugh
Learn a New Language

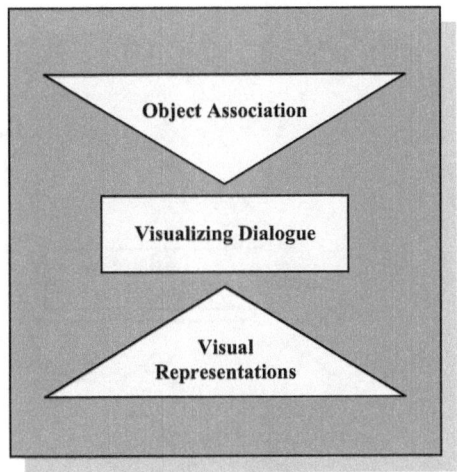

Chapter Three – Visualizing Social Interactions…

To a certain extent we instinctually visualize some of our conversations. Talking and interacting with others is a dance, an "ebb and flow" of information. However, conversations involve so much more than just what is coming out of a person's mouth. It is also about what a person physically does as well. Their gestures and nonverbal queues provide a mountain of information that helps to frame a conversation. Taken together, a mental picture can be formed. We are looking for ways to help us define and visualize a conversation in such a way that we can mentally view and rotate conversations. While chapter three emphasizes social interactions from a more personal point of view, it can also be applied from a professional perspective.

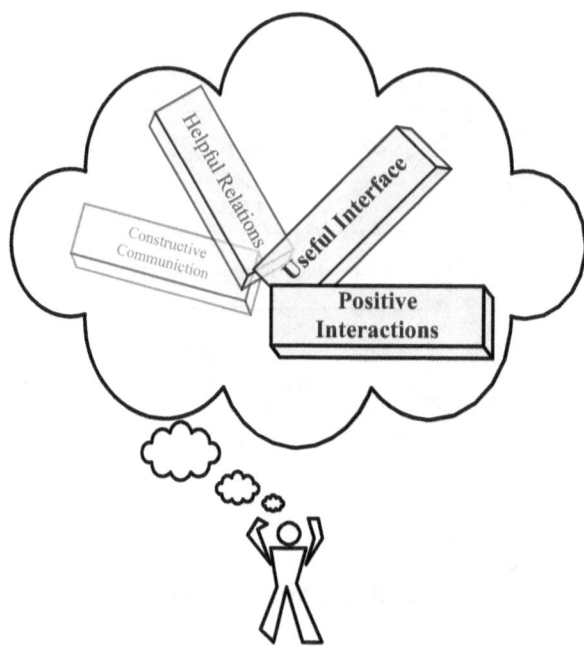

Let's look at some simple ways to view conversations through various scenarios of argument and persuasion. In many conversations, especially professional, we are focused on trying to make a point. More importantly we get caught up in trying to make our points known to all who we believe to be listening. We sometimes talk just to hear our own voice, or we speak louder for authority's sake, or we just plain keep talking to keep others from talking. All of which are bad.

Visualizing social dialogue starts with object association. This mental process correlates shapes with terms that are discussed in conversations. This allows us to visualize how other terms impact the subject. For starters, let us take a look at the "rainbow ruse". It is a common magic trick used to lead a person down two paths that both make sense. They are especially prevalent in horoscopes and "ghost reading" television programs.

The Rainbow Ruse:

"You are shy and are often quiet, yet, you can sometimes be the life of a party".

We have to be careful because a rainbow ruse is a "three-faced" statement. It can apply to people that are shy, people that are outgoing, or people that view themselves as being somewhere in the middle. A good way to visually represent the dialogue is to "box" the concepts.

You are shy and are often quiet...	...yet...	...you can sometimes be the life of a party.

Once we compartmentalized the subjects, we are now able to make adjustments. For example, if we want to cleave the concepts, then we can achieve this by creating a wedge that disconnects the two subjects.

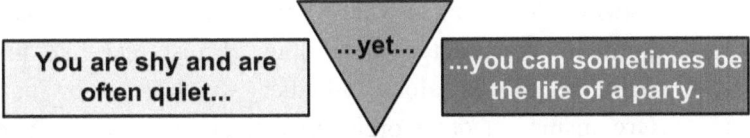

What we are doing is formulating a way to visualize the conversation occurring both from our perspective and outside perspectives. We are not attempting to ascertain the validity of the argument. Instead, we are emphasizing how to visually represent the abstractness of social interactions.

Visualizing the conversation helps to frame our thoughts before we speak. Remember the old adage "engage brain before speaking"? Well in this case we are truly striving to become more measured and less reactionary when it comes to social dialogue.

This is just a simple exercise, yet how about situations that are more complex? How do we approach dynamic dialogue in such a way that we can adequately keep track of many multiple topics? In these cases we "aggregate" the conversations and establish a "visual queue" to help index the conversations.

To illustrate, let us review a more complex concept with a philosophical argument in the following conversation:

> *Setting the Stage:* Laura and her friend are working on a school project together. They have been working on the project for a philosophy class and are currently having a heated discussion on an important piece of their research.
>
> **Ken** – Laura, I am really frustrated. I can't believe that you feel like evil doesn't exist in the universe.
>
> **Laura** – Well this is what I am trying to say…evil is a humanly constructed institution. I just feel like the universe moves along whether we like it or not. Organisms eat other organisms, tigers eat gazelles and humans eat cows. From my perspective, good and evil is just a moral concept created by humans. It doesn't exist.
>
> **Ken** – No, that is not possible. The universe has a morality. Just because the concept of good and evil is defined by humanity, doesn't mean it doesn't exist in a broader context.
>
> **Laura** – Okay, look at it this way. For many various reasons, we know that many millions of animals have

gone extinct on planet earth. We know that dinosaurs were wiped clean off the planet. Do we agree that the mass extinction of any animal species is evil?

Ken – Yes, I do agree with this assessment.

Laura – If we agree that the extinction of the dinosaurs was evil, do you also agree that the extinction of the dinosaurs cleared the path for mammals to evolve?

Ken – Yes, there is a lot of evidence to suggest mammals were allowed to grow and thrive due to the extinction of the dinosaurs.

Laura –Well, humans are mammals. This means that our very existence is predicated on an evil foundation. Can you accept this? Or do you accept that the extinction of the dinosaurs was a good thing?

Ken – I believe that the two events are exclusive of each other. While it is evil that dinosaurs became extinct, it is not our burden to bear. These are separate events.

Laura – Ah, but they are not exclusive of each other, one cannot exist without the other….there is a clearly defined relationship between these two events. If the universe has a morality, how is this defined? My friend with the utmost respect I say this. If the universe has a morality it is truly nebulous and ill-conceived. Why build a sun that will eventually destroy all life on earth?

As we read the exchange of information between Laura and Ken we may have noticed a couple things happening. First, as we read through the dialogue some of us may have become utterly confused with the back and forth. Second, there are "shadow topics" that are lurking within the dialogue. These shadow topics inhibit our ability to glean information from the bigger topics. As a result, we have to aggregate the key topics and create a visual queue. Let us start with the overall topic being discussed:

Next, as we delve a little deeper through the dialogue we get additional clues about the key stakeholders:

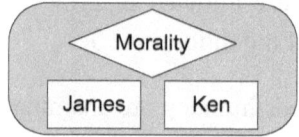

Now let us reflect on our own thought process for a moment to answer a few questions.

- Did we stop to address the moral implications of the discussion?
- Did we get hung up in the details?
- Did we immediately try to form an opinion?

If we answered yes to any one of the above then we might have been finding ourselves struggling to make sense of the conversation due to our own frame of reference. Some of us would have immediately tried to morally dissect the dialogue. Others may have tried to immediately form an opinion. Consequently, we may have spent more time trying to solve the problem instead of just trying to understand the discussion. Remember we want to clear out old thinking, habits and biases.

Next, we want to discern stakeholder positions:

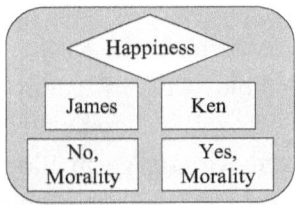

The idea is not to get stuck in the thick of the details. So much of our spoken dialogue is a ruse (i.e. the shadow topics). In visualizing our social interactions, we are trying to discern the root meaning of concepts and the discussion at hand. This means that we should always have a base framework to work with as we approach social interactions. This framework can be unique to each individual. For starters a framework should consist of the following: theme, stakeholders, positions, outcomes and backdrops (aka shadow topics). Taking this framework into account, our thought experiment can be visually represented in the following way:

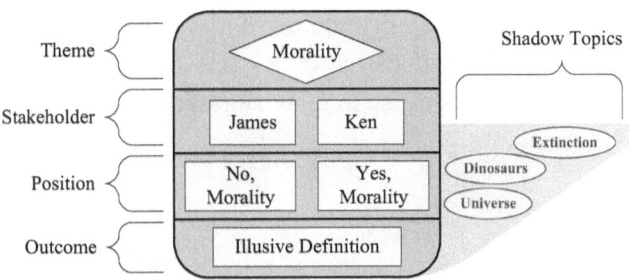

This is just a sample. We could create a visual queue any number of ways. At a minimum we should have a system that captures our important points. The main goal behind developing a visual queue is to create a system that is quick and executable.

Visual Representations…

In almost every possible way, by nature we are victims of irrational behavior. After all we are human. Try as we might to be logical and rational we engage in illogical behavior. The trick is to keep this behavior from becoming chronic. And to help us along in this process, we need to arm ourselves with a way to "see" fallacies as they occur. The more we recognize these logical mishaps the better we get at keeping ourselves from committing the same.

Correlation means Causation…

This is a very common trap. As humans we love to simplify complex terms and in so doing we can sometimes make incorrect correlations between true cause and effect. A good way to visualize this logical error is by correlating the decline of "steam engines" with the growth of "television sets":

"The number of steam engines has declined since the early 1900s. The number of television sets has increased since the early 1900s. Thus, a rise in television sets correlates to a decline in steam engines."

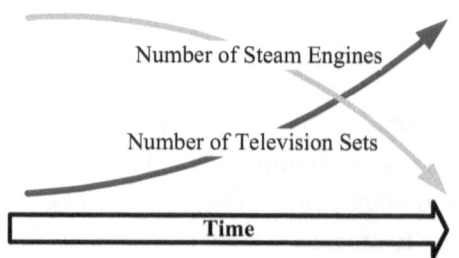

Of course we know this not to be true. It does not make a lot of sense when we think about it in more detail. Putting illogical thoughts into a visual form can really help to highlight what initially appears to be otherwise benign dialogue. So when we come across these types of situations, we should illustrate the dilemma for all to see.

Van Gogh Fallacy…

This logical error tries to normalize "outliers of information". It is essentially a position that we sometimes take when we want an extreme position to seem reasonable.

"Van Gogh was a great artist who lived his life in obscurity. Therefore most great artists are living in obscurity today."

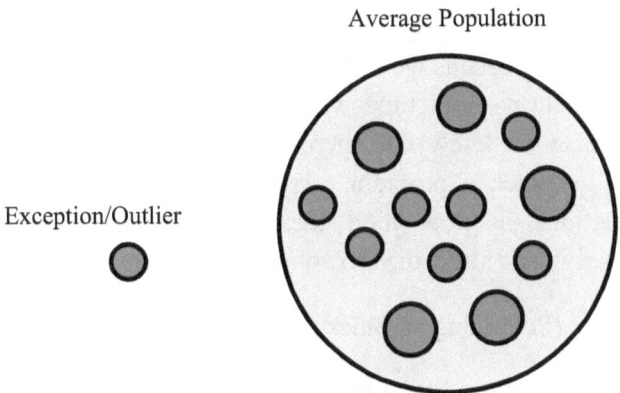

In this case, the statement is trying to make it look like all great artists are living in obscurity. Another way to look at this is from a "minimization" perspective. When we minimize a topic or situation, we are trying to play down the outliers in an effort to make it appear normal.

False Dilemma…

The False Dilemma is probably one of the most common mistakes we come across in office meetings. How many times have we heard in a meeting that "We only have two options:

option 1 or option 2". The statement is intended to narrow the topic list and it is usually done in an extreme way so as to give the audience a feeling that only these options can be considered. It also infers that all other options have been considered when in fact they have not:

"Either you are with us, or you are with the terrorists."[8]

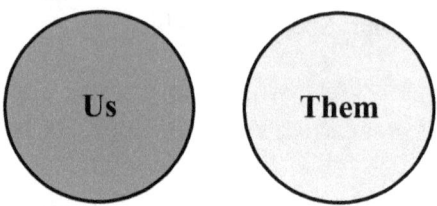

For obvious reasons we know this to be incorrect. In the heat of the moment we sometimes view these statements as reasonable. Of course we know that there are more than just a couple of ways to attack a problem. When faced with these types of interactions it is a good idea to speak up, highlight the alternative and show the crowd more perspective.

Splitting (Polarizing or Black-and-White)…

Splitting is a form of the False Dilemma fallacy. These kinds of statements are usually associated with people called the "doctors of death". This type of thinking is an "all or nothing" style. A splitter leaves a very distinct social signature. They will frequently make use of words like "never" and "always". They may see a single unpleasant event as a never-ending pattern of defeat. We can visualize this like cutting firewood:

"I scored 900 on my SAT, I am never going to college!"

---

[8] George Walker Bush, US President 2001-2009, Transcript of President Bush's address, September 20th 2001

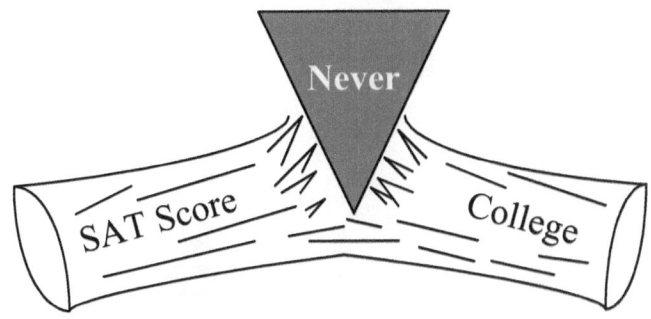

In this case, the word "never" becomes an enduring fixture that lodges into ideas. It does not separate, or decouple the wood. It is dangerous for a number of reasons. First, it is hard to remove negative thinking once it gets lodged into the discussion. Second, splitters will over time socially construct their own realities. When we approach situations with an "all or nothing" attitude we inhibit our own ability to see other angles, attitudes and opinions. Eventually, we only recognize negative events in our life as being the ONLY events that occur in our lives. Consequently we overlook positive perspectives because we spend so much time focused on the negative perspectives. Instead, we need to realize that the world is not purely "good" and "evil", or "black" and "white". The world is so much more complex. Sometimes we forget that the world shouts out at us in color.

Argument by Generalization…

At some point in our day-to-day conversations, we engage in a bit of generalization. It is not all together unhealthy; our need to generalize is a way to help aggregate information. Our brains want to simplify terms and concepts and to a certain degree we take this for granted. We are especially big offenders of this when it comes to grouping people of different cultures or abilities. Argument by Generalization is similar to the Van

Gogh Fallacy, but it works in reverse. We view ourselves as the rule that everyone else should be measured by.

"I can handle my alcohol; therefore everyone should be able to handle their alcohol."

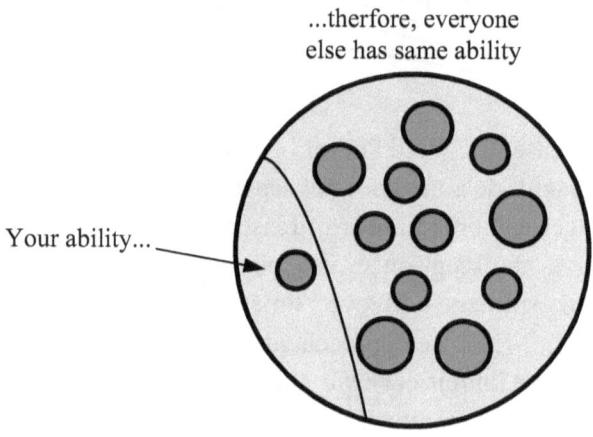

...therfore, everyone else has same ability

Your ability...

In the socio-anthropological circles, this is called ethnocentrism[9]. From a human evolutionary perspective, it is an identity mechanism that we use to help create group identity. This helps to create a direction in group dynamics and ideologies towards a group's own cultural background. We try to equate various phenomenon around us based on the backdrop of information that we currently have available at our fingertips. However, the social groups that we hang out with create biases over time and can sometimes create issues. For example, we cannot make a generalization based on one's own experience and generally apply that broadly across all groups or cultures. Remember our realities are relative and as such cannot be broadly applied. In particular, public politicians are notorious offenders of generalization errors, "I grew up in the heartland of America, and therefore I know what is best for America." In

---

[9] Keyword Internet Search: "Ethnocentric Behavior"

other words, our idea of America equates to everyone's normative view of America?

Misdirection (the Shiny Rocket approach)...

Also called a Red Herring, these social misdeeds can be quite effective. The intent of a "red herring" is to redirect attention to a shiny object that has very little relevance to the topic being discussed:

"Our public school systems have failed our children because our teachers lack empathy. After all, the state's budget is hardly balanced."

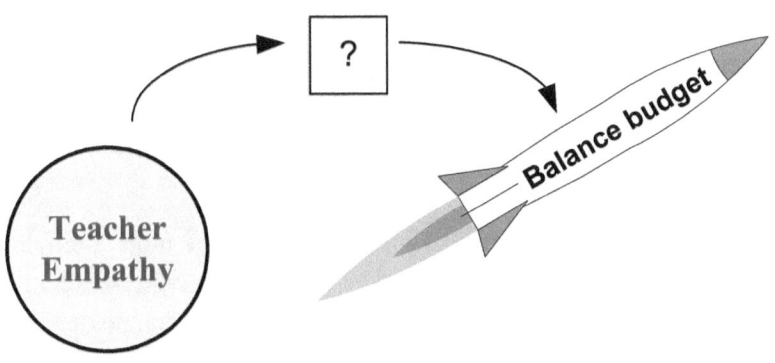

In this case, there is not any evidence linking the state's budget to a teacher's lack of empathy for the children. A crowd can become fixated on the bigger and brighter object. Red herrings are especially effective when they are more subtle.

Gray Herring...

A Gray Herring is a more subtle form of a Red Herring. It is harder to detect and is especially prevalent when subjects become technical:

"Statistics show that customers are more inclined to bank online. After all, statistical models have not proven that the government should have more regulations."

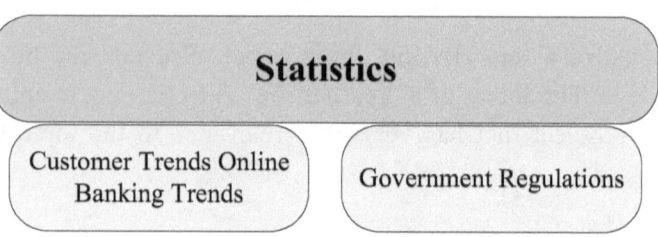

This is a more complicated case where the word "statistics" is used as a grey herring to highlight an official sounding word like "statistics" in one sentence and referring to "statistics" in another sentence. While sounding official, no correlation is offered between online banking trends and government regulation discussions.

Argument from Authority…

Argument from Authority is probably one of the more annoying arguments that people can make. This argument works in a couple different ways. The first, is when people "name drop" to use someone else's credentials to help bolster their argument. The second is when someone uses their own credentials to strengthen an argument.

Name Droppers: "Trust me…my cousin is a CPA."

MD Complex: "Trust me…I am a doctor."

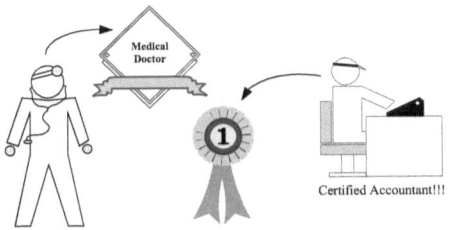

In these cases, people do not draw attention to their knowledge base, rather these people short circuit a conversation by drawing attention to their authority, prestige, or association. Fortunately, this is something that is easily disarmed with a "second opinion" of authority. We should not blindly accept second hand information, or even information that is derived from a single source.

Conclusion...

The amount of "logical fallacies" is endless. There are numerous websites and books[10] dedicated to logical fallacies. Seeing logical errors in conversation is great because they lend themselves so well to visual representations. Our goal is to practice and develop these visual representations in our day-to-day conversations as they occur. It is also helpful to lookup these other common conversational errors online. Take some time to diagram out other common errors. It takes practice. Even understanding a handful of these errors are helpful and will go a long way in formalizing our visual thought processes.

---

[10] Keyword Internet Search: "Logical Fallacies" + "Examples"

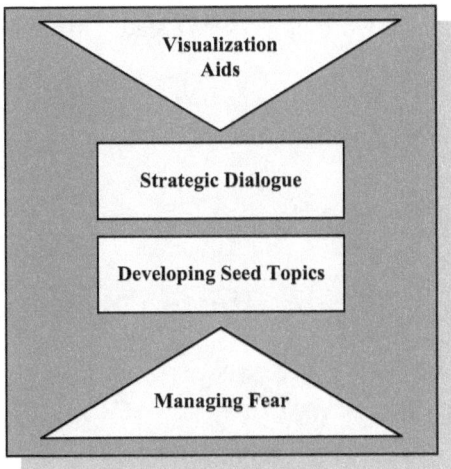

Chapter Four – Constructive Visualization Aids...

Learning a spoken language is no easy task. Accordingly, it is not so difficult to see how "specialized language" further complicates the communication process. Employing visualization aids in both our social dialogue as well as our surroundings helps us to make sense of these more specialized concepts. Turning social interactions into visual objects gives us something more tangible to rotate and manipulate. We will explore different ways to help visualize and organize these abstracts parts of our dialogue.

Word Clouds...

Word clouds are helpful in representing the number of times a word, or topic, occurs in a conversation. Word clouds are useful in steering difficult to understand, or nebulous, discussions. They are also great at formulating the high-level details for project roadmaps. Word clouds can be created by keeping track the number of times a topic comes up in a discussion. They can also be created from our notes via online programs. As an example, a generic word cloud was created using an online word cloud program.[11]

This particular method of visualization helps to narrow the focus for major topics being discussed. There are different ways word clouds can be represented (simple, round, square, vertical, or horizontal), however, it is best to keep word clouds simple and elegant. As a discussion (or project) matures word clouds should be less emphasized. Therefore, it is a good idea to use word clouds early on in social interactions to help stimulate dialogue, create agendas, or outline projects.

Topic Modeling…

Topic modeling is similar to word clouds. However, the difference is seen in the level of details. Topic models emphasize the bigger and more critical items contained within a word cloud. In addition, topic modeling is best used in interactive sessions. This is similar to brainstorming, but instead we keep talking points limited to high-level topics. For best results, topic modeling session should be viewed as a two step

---

[11] Keyword Internet Search: "Free" + "Online Word Cloud Generator"

process: the first session is the "all-in" phase; the second session is the "grouping phase".

1. The first step is to allow everyone to put up whatever topic they feel. It is critical that the first phase be free of ANY criticism. In other words, people need to feel comfortable with sharing ideas without fear of criticism. The only stipulation in the first step is that topics need to be "headlines". We want to keep the ideas between two and four words. We do not want to get caught up in details, and sticking to "headlines" helps to keep conversations fluid.
2. Next, we have the "grouping phase". We want to focus on taking our basic headlines and grouping them by themes or genres. But the key to effective topic modeling is to ensure that it is a collaborative effort.

While word clouds are great as a topic identification tool in a conversation, or document, they have less utility as interactions move into increasing levels of details. Topic models have more definition and are a little more actionable than word clouds. Using our earlier word cloud topics as an example, our topic model would look something like this:

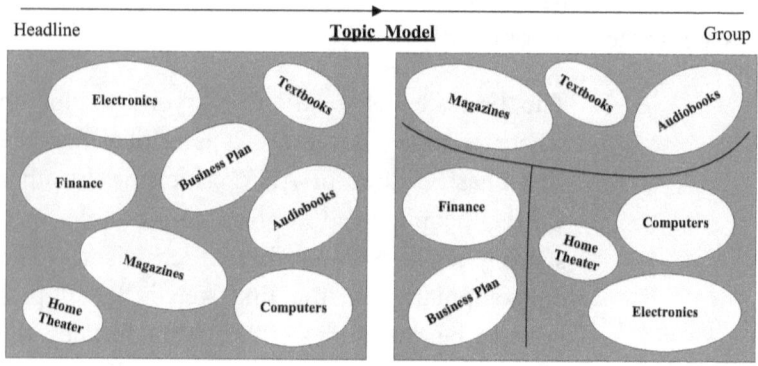

While topic models are great for just about any occasion, they are especially useful in bridging word clouds with roadmaps.

Roadmaps...

Roadmaps can range from very simple to extremely complex. Building on what we have created in our topic model, we are now looking to organize our ideas into actionable outputs. In this case, we can use the roadmap to help organize our thoughts from multiple perspectives. We could use our roadmap to get the basics of a business model together. We could also use this as a way to create a website, or to organize a blog. A roadmap is utilized to visually convey a direction of ideas (i.e. where we are now versus where we want to be in the future).

Roadmap

As more ideas are incorporated, more "forks" in the road can be considered for inclusion in the roadmap. We can also view roadmaps in the way we travel for vacations. When we plan our vacations we seldom just jump in our cars and leave for a week.

To a certain extent we plan this out. We might consider bathroom breaks, food and gas stops, alternate routes, and points of interest. In a way, planning a vacation is just as complicated as planning for business at work.

Strategic Dialogue: Word Cloud – Topic Model – Roadmap

When we put the last three tools together we get a nice social package that we can leverage in a strategic way. While we could certainly see value in these social interaction in our professional environment, there is no reason why we cannot also leverage these strategies in our personal endeavors. For example: completing college, personal finances, retirement strategies, family dilemmas and home building projects.

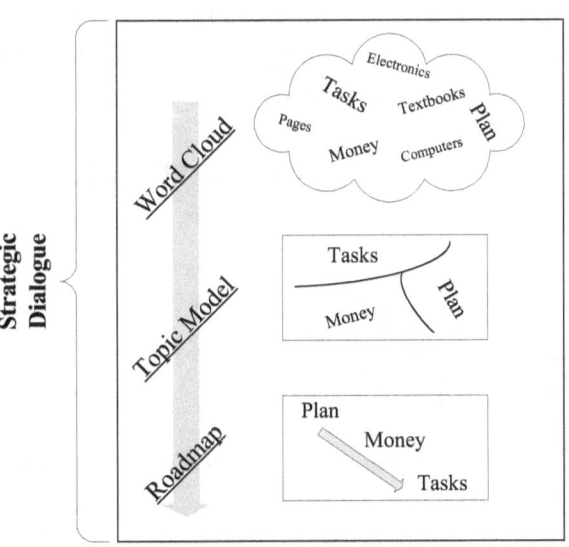

Strategic dialogue takes grand political posturing in an organization and turns them into operational and actionable work items. From the political to the tactical, we refer to this in total as the "Level of Dialogue" which will be covered in Chapter Seven.

Information Filtering…

Another constructive tool that we should exercise on a daily basis is "Information Filtering". We want to constantly be asking ourselves what information is appropriate given the social setting and subject. This has applicability to both our professional and personal settings. To help visualize this, we have to filter information in a "vertical" and "horizontal" fashion. When we say "vertical" we are talking about the hierarchy, or level of information in a specific domain. When we say "horizontal" we are talking about information that crosses the vertical information domains. For example, microeconomics, macroeconomics, positive and normative economics would all be topics that fall into a vertical "economics" domain. Horizontally speaking, mathematics (algebra, statistics, and calculus, etc…) would be a domain that crosses many multiple domains.

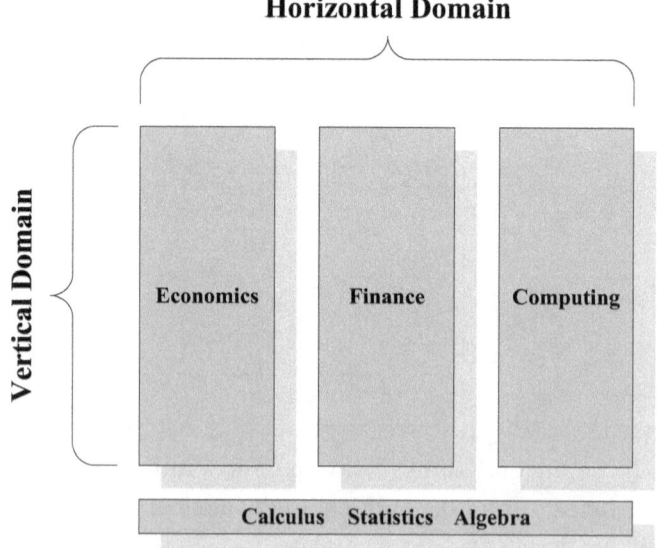

For a number of reasons, this is a critical point that must not be underestimated. We want to understand not only the application of knowledge vertically in a domain but how other information domains apply to other information domains.

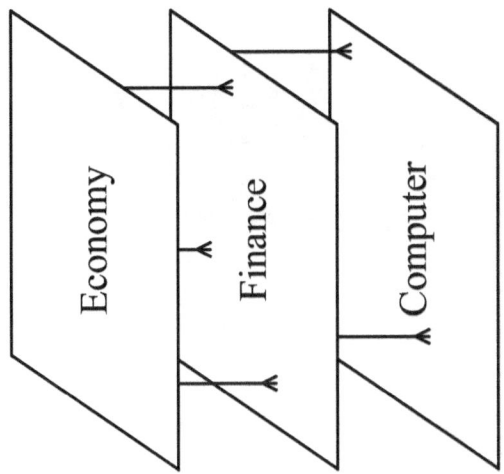

From an information filter perspective, we want to make sure that when we are engaged in social interactions, we want to understand how best to "filter" information both incoming and outgoing.

Lastly, we need to understand that an information domain can also be rotated into its own verticality. For example, using the figure from above, we can certainly view mathematics as a horizontal domain, yet we could just as easily rotate the diagram to make mathematics a vertical domain as well.

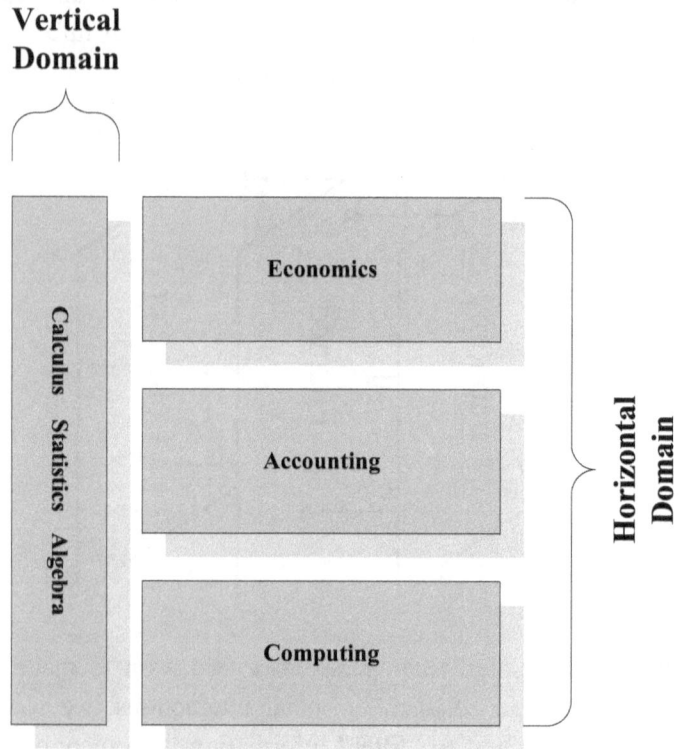

The rotational nature of information domains simply means that we live in a fully matrixed environment. As a result, we have to be comfortable in manipulating and rotating the way we view the exchange of information around us. In other words, we have to be comfortable with change.

Parry and Counter…

Parry and counter can be viewed exactly as it sounds. The idea here is to subtly agree in part to dialogue being directed at us. Most notably is when we are being criticized. Our immediate response is to become defensive. We cross our arms, furrow our eyebrows, and use words that do not exist in the dictionary like "ah huh" or "hmm". This usually indicates that we are not really listening to criticism, but waiting for our turn to talk and defend ourselves. Without a doubt, we want to avoid defensive behavior (which we will cover in Chapter Eight). At the same time, we are seeing ourselves as experts with valid opinions to offer. So we want to show our perspective in an attentive way while also considering other points of view (valid, or invalid, as they may be). A parry and counter is a social maneuver that essentially gives us an ability to acknowledge other points while at the same time circling back to our main points. This occurs in two parts:

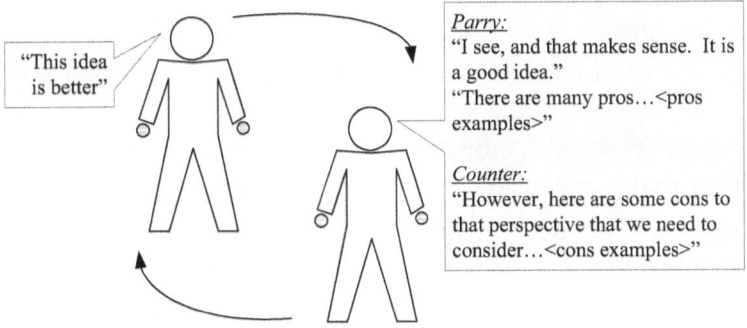

Parry and counter techniques work effectively when we are very knowledgeable on a subject. Also, people love to be validated and a well constructed parry serves this purpose rather nicely. However, if we execute this strategy with very little awareness of the topic at hand, our counter will come off as being weak and you will in turn run the risk of being viewed negatively. As we practice this maneuver, we will find increasingly creative ways to work the parry and counter strategy.

Gracious Exits…

A gracious exit is an attrition limiting maneuver. When our parry and counter fails, we need to graciously exit, or concede the point. There are times when we need to concede or exit a conversation because we either have conflicts of interest, or because we are not that knowledgeable on a particular subject. There is a process to conceding a topic or point. In order to save ourselves further embarrassment, it is better to graciously exit when we get ourselves into a bind, either socially or technically. At least in this way it highlights our social competence in understanding that "we don't know what we don't know". In some cases people will appreciate this behavior more versus trying to clobber together a poorly formed thought.

Here is another way to think about it. Imagine that we are the head coach of a pro sports team. We are in a heated battle with the other team. We lose by a couple points, but it does not matter…we have lost the game. The winning head coach comes up to shake our hand. Instead of giving him a "good game handshake" we turn the other way and head to the locker room. No doubt, this is unsportsmanlike conduct. But now imagine all the bystanders who are watching this transpire. Can we envision how they would react to this exchange?

Okay now, take that visual and translate that to a board meeting. We are in the middle of some challenging dialogue and can no longer maintain our position. Imagine being the person that does not graciously concede the point in a board meeting. Now imagine how we are viewed among all the other people in the crowd? Our initial thought is that we do not want to appear weak...but if our position is already weakened, we only continue to do ourselves considerably more public relations damage by not conceding a weak point. It is better to graciously concede the point, jump on board with the new idea and help to make a strong idea even stronger.

"What do you think of my plan?"

"Excellent idea, what can I do to help?"

Check Dancing...

Check dancing is the art of paying a bill. Engaging in a check dance is proper etiquette, and should ALWAYS be practiced regardless of the situation. Individuals who do not "check dance" just come off as being crass. While we typically see this in restaurant situations, it can be applied to any "group spending" activities. We have to remember that this process is not just a "monetary haggling" exercise, more importantly this is a "social contracting" exercise.

Imagine we are out on a "couples date". We have wrapped up a great evening. Good conversation, many laughs. Then the bill shows up at the table. Between all parties the bill looks pretty hefty. The other couple offers to pick up the tab. We exchange a look of awkward silence...but we decide to keep quiet. No check dancing. The evening eventually comes to a close, and then the after party "hot wash meeting" begins.

Our hot wash meeting might go something like this, "…that was a good evening…we had some great conversations…I am so glad that they picked up the bill…we could not afford to pickup that entire bill…"

Remember, for right or wrong, we are publicly being judged and the other couple will also hold their own hot wash meeting. Their meeting might go something like this, "…nice evening…there was some good conversation…but can you believe they didn't even offer to pay up for dinner? So rude…we won't be going out to dinner with them again…"

For etiquette's sake we need to engage in a check dance. We do not necessarily have to pay for the entire bill, but the mere exercise of hashing out the details is required decorum. A better way to handle a check dance is to plan a paycheck ahead. Set some money aside so that when the situation comes up again, we can check dance with confidence.

Mirroring…

Imitation is the best form of flattery. Mirroring is a common technique that many of us employ instinctually. After all we learn to emulate our parents at a very young age. Accordingly, humans are well equipped to recognize signs of displeasure in those we admire. Our ability to mirror others around us stems from our need to be acknowledged. It is born out of our praise seeking behavior. Consequently, there are a lot of social pathologies that can sprout from this behavior. However, that topic could fill up an entire book. Mirroring, when approached deliberately, can be a great social tool.

Mirroring has a level of applicability, and can be generally categorized into "micro-mirroring" and "macro-mirroring" behavior. Micro-mirroring behavior is more stealthy and subtle. For example, speaking volume, posture, head tilts, eye gazes, and other non-verbal gestures are all examples of micro-mirroring behavior. If someone is soft-spoken, then we become soft-spoken. If someone crosses their leg, then we cross our leg. Micro-mirroring is a subtle mechanism that helps to cultivate harmonization between two or more parties. On the opposite end, we have "macro-mirroring" behavior and it is the opposite of subtle. Macro-mirroring behavior encompasses much larger, and riskier, behavior. This can include altering our physical appearance, clothes, hair, cars, houses, and even our financial spending (i.e. "Keeping up with the Joneses").

As one can imagine we cannot just broadly apply mirroring techniques in our day-to-day interactions. We need an application guideline that makes mirroring more deliberate and targeted.

For the general population, the mirroring magnitude is inversely proportional to its effectiveness. In other words, "micro-mirroring" behavior is less risky, and more likely to be successfully applied given the social situation.

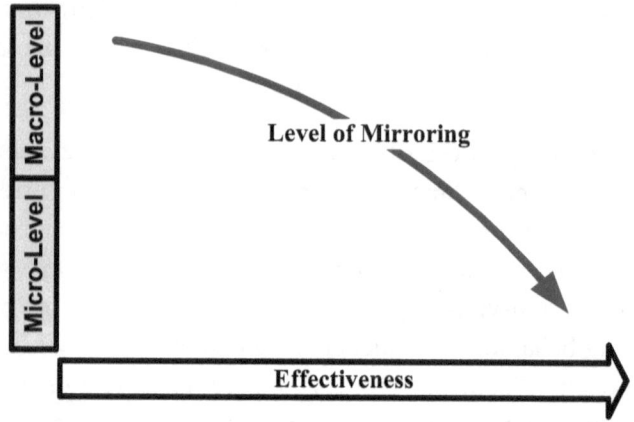

On the flipside, macro-mirroring effectiveness is directly proportional to the narcissistic level of the targeted individual. For example, an extremely narcissistic neighbor will respond more favorably to mirroring that approximates the macro level. Not sure if this makes sense? Well, it is kind of why we have neighborhoods. If we are the only person on the block driving a high end luxury car, then chances are good that we are not well liked. On the flip side, if we happen to live in a neighborhood where we are the only person not driving a luxury car, then we might be shunned. Same applies to work, but instead of neighborhoods, we have "departments".

When applied deliberately, micro-mirroring is a good technique. This is not to say that we should not speak our minds. On the contrary, we need to be comfortable in exchanging our own points of views. Remember, when we talk about "mirroring behavior" we are not necessarily focused on "the content of what we say", rather we are focused on "our external behavior" outside of what we say. Which brings us to our final point, beware of macro-mirroring. It is a dangerous game to be doing things for the sake of others and not ourselves.

Seed Topics (Conversation Starters)…

Seed topics are good to have on hand as conversation starters. Like starting a fire, we need to have two types of wood: kindling (light wood) and logs (bulk wood). Quite literally in conversation, we need to have the very same outlook in starting conversations. Unless we are lucky, we will not get a fire started by directly lighting heavy logs first. Instead we start fires with lighter twigs and sticks (i.e. kindling). This helps to cultivate the fire and get it prepped for the larger logs and the same goes for conversations.

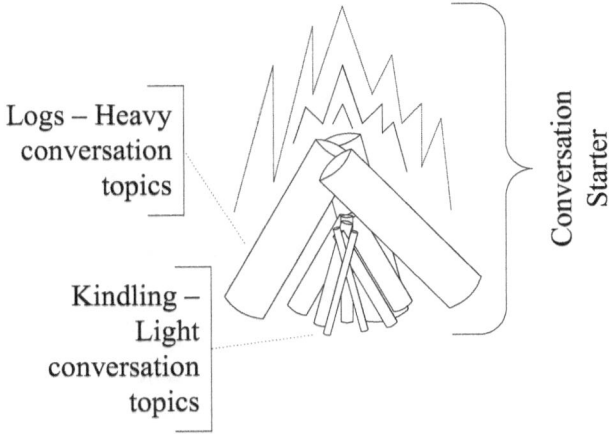

From a social perspective, our seed topics come in various forms and levels. We are all smart people. We have a great deal of acquired knowledge that we have built up over our lifetimes. Remember we have become hyper-specialized as a society. Unfortunately, this stacks the deck against us as we have a natural tendency to over emphasize our own knowledge base when engaged in conversations. We have a penchant for shifting our conversations towards a form that is more comfortable to us. This is understandable as our own communication style is filled with specialized facts about the world. Generally speaking, this is a conversation style that is of interest to one person…our self. It is a language that we have developed and a language that we understand. Simply stated, starting a fire with heavy, or specialized topics, is a good way to not achieve ignition in a conversation.

Developing Seed Topics…

First, we have to take an interest in the world around us and in other topics that might not be at the top of our list. We need to realize that we have to cultivate a variety of topics. This is hard to achieve if we are stuck in the "Country of Me" mentality.

To see where we are coming from we need to bring another short story about John back into the picture.

Mary's Outreach…

Mary learned after many years of working in the trenches with a variety of people and organizations that it was a good idea to have "portable topics" that are relatable to just about anybody she came into contact with. In this case, Mary leveraged topics that centered on local geographies. In particular, Mary extended this knowledge domain to encompass more about the local colleges in a particular region of the country and world.

In one particular instance, Mary bumped into someone who was from Wisconsin. Her mental rolodex ran through the two major colleges in the area: University of Wisconsin and Marquette University. So instead of jumping into the obvious "cheese" and "football" comments…Mary's comments about the local universities spoke to this person on a deeper level.

Utilizing local events, Mary was also familiar with a large air show that they have up in Wisconsin (Oshkosh). Mary is careful to allow this person from Wisconsin to be in command of the topics. She is allowing information from others to come to her direction, versus the other way around. Lastly, Mary's usage of this particular "seed topic" is something that we can all relate too.

Light Seed Topics: (kindling)

- Local Geographies: Festivals, Universities, etc…
- Global Events: Local and Regional
- Popular Culture: Entertainment, Music, Movies, etc…
- Fashion Trends: Shoes, Clothes, etc…
- Sports and Sporting Events

Heavy Seed Topics: (bulk)

- Physics
- Mathematics
- History
- Medicine
- Law
- Religion
- Politics

Heavy seed topics are very specialized and when we initially meet people for the first time we want to be friendly and cordial. These heavy seed topics are to be avoided for two reasons. First, these seed topics stimulate competitive conversational interactions. Second, heavy topics can mentally turn off our logical brain functions by routing our thoughts through a more emotional channel within our brain functioning.[12]

The "heavy conversationalist" can stimulate a wide variety of emotional triggers. From fear to ambivalence, an emotional

---

[12] Keyword Internet Search: "Short Term" + "Cognitive Benefits"

trigger can be hard to shake and can lead us into a logical fog that is difficult to clear. As social interactionists we need to understand how to cultivate social handshakes with people that we meet. We do not want to arouse emotional triggers in others or ourselves. These types of triggers can lead us down into very emotional territory.

Understanding Fear…

Fear is an interesting phenomenon. Socially speaking, fear can incapacitate a person. We are often times stopped dead in our tracks when it comes to experiencing fear. From a threatening boss to a large xenomorph in our bed room, processing fear leaves little room for logic and rationality in the brain. Fear is the "logical mind killer", but this is for good reason.[13]

Back in the Day: Idaltu John…

Let us imagine John back in time, 200,000 years. John is sitting on a rock outcropping. It is a sunny day, not a cloud in the big blue sky. The air is crisp. John is by himself not to far away from the fire and the rest of the group. He kneels down to inspect some recent game tracks. As he tries to surmise where the tracks are leading off, a shadow comes up from behind. John's brain is able to process a rough shape of what appears to be a big bear. His fight-or-flight response kicks in, and his brain makes a snap decision. This is a very large animal. It is time to run very fast. His body takes over and his cardiopulmonary functions skyrocket. John takes a dive off the rock outcropping to the forest floor about 6 feet below and runs off into the thicker forest ahead.

John runs for about 500 feet and begins to slow his pace. His acute stress response begins to subside. He becomes as still as

---

[13] Keyword Internet Search: "Flight or Fight Response"

the trees. John visually scans the surroundings. He is careful not take another step. John's breathing rhythm comes under control. He does not make a sound. He strains to detect any faint branch cracking. After waiting, John's brain signals that he is out of immediate danger. He tentatively and very deliberately walks back to camp. John is careful to avoid the last location of the incident. He lives to see another day.

Analysis of Fear...

Our fight-or-flight response is pivotal to our survival. Not just humans, but all animals. Imagine if John decided to take time out of that situation to determine the validity of the threat. We only have fractions of a second, and if we take too much time to logically work out a problem we might end up as another animal's next meal. Consequently, we have deeply programmed responses to externally perceived dangers.

Since we are not being chased by bears or wolves, one would think that our sympathetic pathways are evoked less these days. However, this is not the case, to a certain extent these pathways are overloaded and overexcited. Not only do we still have to deal with the natural elements of the world (e.g. rain, hurricanes, tornadoes, spiders, bears, snakes, wolves, etc...), we now have to deal with manufactured elements of the world (e.g. cars, trains, airplanes, jobs, etc...). Fear has survived because it promotes survival. If we fail to react to perceived threats around us we could end up becoming dinner on the game reserve. Our brains are wired to flinch first and ask questions later.

In the modern world it is deceptively simple to activate our fear response (e.g. an email from the boss that says simply, "Come See Me Please"). As cognitive thinkers our panic attacks will typically drive us to frantically search for the source of a threat. When we cannot quantify, or qualify, the threat we then begin to over interpret our fears as being irrational.[14] Consequently, we misconstrue and overly "personalize our defectiveness" (e.g. "I am going crazy!", "What did I do?!", "I am a lunatic!"). We are rational human beings, but we are easily susceptible to conditioning. We are not perfect, we make mistakes. But over time, when taken to extremes, we can easily turn normal behavior into our worst enemy.

It is helpful to understand that we fail as human beings. Whether we like it or not, we fail. Accepting failure is good.   At the same time, we do not want to be a victim of history. So for us to grow socially (and in general) we have to learn to accept our failing while at the same time not dwelling on the past. We also need to understand where are behavioral bottlenecks are in life (Chapter 5, Behavioral Strings). So much of our anxiety and fears can be mitigated by detangling, and simplifying, our life agendas.

Conclusion...

From strategic dialogue to managing fear, visualization aids can be used with great success in aiding our social interactions. It is especially helpful to understand the layering aspect of social interactions.   Furthermore, it is helpful to understand the links between the layers. Seeing the social world around us from this perspective will go a long way in making us a more effective communicator.

---

[14] Keyword Internet Search: "Panic Control" + "Irrational"

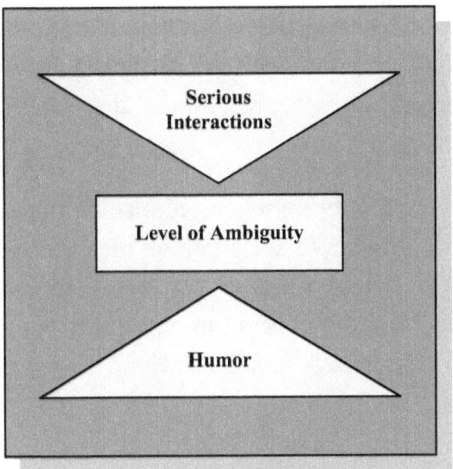

Chapter Five – Extremes: Interrogations & Comedy

While we have talked about horizontal and vertical information domains, social interactions can also be organized according to their level of "seriousness". From extremely intense to light hearted humor, our social interactions are quite complex. While most of our day-to-day discussions fall in between these extremes, it is worth adding in some additional perspective about social activities that occur out on the fringes.

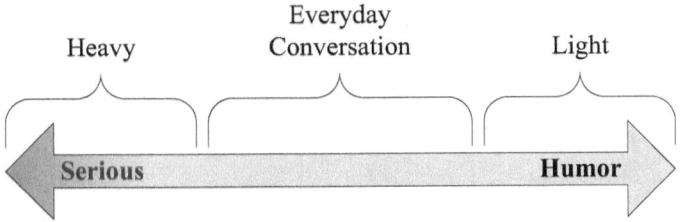

Serious conversations are usually undertaken in an effort to resolve ambiguity. For example, military command and control systems cannot be ambiguous. The information has to be precise and well defined. Another example of this can be seen in medical delivery systems. When we walk into a hospital there is an amazing amount of seriousness that goes on behind the scenes to make sure people get what they need.

On the opposite end of the spectrum, light hearted conversations are more ambiguous. In light hearted discussions we leave room for concepts to grow. We are given an idea that leaves us to fill in the blanks. Light hearted conversations are like social "treasure hunts" and the concept of ambiguity is the catalyst that drives this process along. It is also what makes lighter dialogue so much fun.

Interrogations: The Darker Side…

Paramilitary (Police) and Military interrogations techniques are fascinating research topics that provide extremely useful ways to visually represent social interactions. For sure, we do not want to get caught in the cross hairs of a seasoned interrogator. In the military, they are called "human intelligence collectors". It is very useful to see the techniques employed by the "darker side" of the community.

Setting the Stage: Scandalous John…

John works at a machine shop, he has no kids, but he has some family and friends in the local area. He has hit a rough patch in his life and is having trouble with his girlfriend. Professionally, John has been having trouble at work and it has been causing him persistent feelings of anxiety. On a couple of occasions he was admitted to the hospital for panic attacks. After getting off of a particularly brutal work schedule, John and his girlfriend get into a tough discussion about the finances…the discussions starts out rough…it later turns into yelling…the yelling turns into something else…

…a couple weeks later…

John gets called into the local police station for questioning. Since it is a small town the station chief has to call in a specially trained detective from a larger nearby city to help with the investigation.

John is brought in for questioning about the disappearance of his girlfriend. She has not been seen in a couple weeks.

The Interrogation…

John has been read all his rights and decides to move forward without the presence of legal aid. Being a small community, the local station chief and John have a friendly relationship.

- Rapport Building
    - Local Chief: "Hi John how'ya doin?"
    - John: "Not too bad, work has been a little rough."
    - Local Chief: "Oh yeah, what has been happening?"
    - John: "…just been tough…my old manager has me working 12 hour shifts…so I haven't been getting much sleep…"
- Isolation
    - Local Chief: "Well, do you know why we brought you into the station?"
    - John: "No, can't say that I understand what this is all about"
    - Local Chief: "Well, it is about your girlfriend's car…seems to be missing and we are just bringing in people to see what might have happened."

- o John: \<leans back away from table> "...well I don't know anything about it...she left after we had a big argument..."
- o Local Chief: "Well John that is where we have a problem....I have to step out of the room to get some help. I need you to think through the details for me...because I have a friend that I want you to talk to."
- o \<John sits alone for 15 minutes...left to his thoughts...>
- Emotional Fear-Down then Minimization
    - o Interrogator: \<enters the room> "John, I gotta be honest, we know more about what happened to your girlfriend. Is there anything you want to tell us about what REALLY happened?"
    - o John: \<silence>
    - o Interrogator: "Well here is the deal, we have a pretty good understanding of the facts \<reads through folder that is a stack of papers related to another case>...but what we don't know is the timing of what you did the day your girlfriend disappeared..."
    - o John: \<muttering, incoherent>
    - o Interrogator: "Look John, I know this is scary...we got you in the middle of a crime and we understand your background...we totally understand your difficulties at work...it is tough world, these things could happen to anybody..."
    - o John: \<changes posture, leans into the table>
- Appeal to Ego
    - o Interrogator \<senses his posture change>: Here is the deal, you gotta ask yourself what does a MAN have to do in these situations...does he

run from responsibility...or does he tackle his mistakes head on?"

- o John: <grim look...shakes his head...>...it just happened so fast....

In our "straw man" interrogation, John ends up giving the police a confession. Trained interrogators are truly amazing to watch. Every detail is orchestrated: the environment, placement of objects within the environment, the placement of the chairs, inflection in tone, and body movement.

We also want to take some time to understand body language. There were a couple of signs that John was withdrawing (leaning back) from the conversation or reengaging in conversation (leaning towards the table). These are body movements that illustrate a state of mind.

Shifting gears towards the military, the United States Army understands interrogations really well. In this area, the US Army operates from what is known as the Human Intelligence Collector Operations[15] manual. From a visual interactionist perspective, it makes for excellent reading. While we will not be able to cover all the topics, let us review some of the major themes that involve this more subversive line of work.

Direct Approach...

The direct approach is as it sounds. Questions are not ancillary; instead, they are straight to the point. An interrogator will ask direct questions as long as there is reason to believe that the source is answering in a reasonable and truthful manner. The idea is that in many situations, the environment itself is enough

---

[15] Keyword Internet Search: "Human Intelligence" + "Collector Operations" + "FM"

to allow direct questioning to be effective. Where direct questioning is not effective…other techniques must be explored.

Incentive Approach…

The incentive approach is similar to techniques employed by used cars salesman. This approach is based on the interrogator identifying and exploiting a "need" from the source. The source may be interested in material or emotional reward. They may also be looking to have a human or environmental factor "handled". The exchange of goods must be sincere for the effort to work. Humans are pretty smart when it comes to summing up the exchange of goods. Incentives can be small or large and can be combined with a direct approach.

Emotional Approach…

The emotional approach of the US Army manual is by far the "more sneaky" way of dealing with people. It deals with exploiting our emotional wants and needs. Interrogators will use all manner of emotional pressure to breakdown the mind of a person on a very personal level. As we saw in the police example earlier, the interrogator appealed to John's ego to be a man. Emotional approaches can be focused on any number of feelings: hate, revenge, greed or love.

Conclusion of the Dark Side…

Our main purpose is to highlight the social dynamics of how extreme dialogue is used to elicit a response from individuals under extreme circumstances. This is a really important point to understand. While these settings maybe unfamiliar to most, it is not uncommon to see people instinctually employing these techniques in every day social settings. We need to understand that when someone launches a series of interrogation techniques, that we realize it for what it truly is….a tool looking to draw out a specific response from an intended target. Whether it is contract negotiations or a midyear review, our emotions, body movements and posture all have a story to tell to those around us (see Chapter 8). Fear and anxiety are mind killers and we will delve into those inner mechanics in subsequent chapters.

Comedy: The Lighter Side…

Now that we have dissected some elements of "serious conversations", we want to spend time on the lighter side. It is through comedy and humor that we are able to get people to see other perspectives. Where heavy and serious interactions are looking to mitigate ambiguity, lighter conversations are a way to introduce ambiguity.

Comedic dialogue is a perfect example of this phenomenon in action:

> Short Story – Turtle Robs a Bank…
>
> A snail walks into a bank to make a deposit. As the snail completes his business, a turtle comes in and robs the bank.
>
> Afterwards, the police ask the snail to describe what happened, the snail says, 'I have no clue, everything happened so fast!'
>
> Short Story – Farmer Kicks a Snail…
>
> A farmer is roused by something at his door late one winter's night. He opens his door, looks around and looks down and there, at his doorstep, is a snail. The snail says, "Can I come in, I'm really cold?"

The farmer says, "No, get outta here you tiny creature," and kicks the snail into a garden across from the house.

A year passes by and it is winter again. The farmer hears a sound at his door. He opens the door, looks around and sees the same snail from last year, who says, "What did you do that for?"

Think back to the last time someone told us a joke….now think back to when we did not "get" the joke. When someone had to "spell out" the premise of the joke (i.e. making a joke unambiguous), then it no longer becomes funny.

Comedy frequently contains unexpected shifts in perspective. This is a fundamental point of comedic dialogue. Comedy helps to alleviate the seriousness of unambiguous situations by allowing "hard and fast" facts to be molded into a different perspective so that we can see that we are all dealing with the same challenges.

The lighter side of comedy can be organized in a number of ways. While interrogators are working the individuals, comedians are working the crowd. The level of ambiguity has to rise with the number of people we are talking to. This is not isolated to comedy, this also applies to politicians (however, that is a different topic entirely).

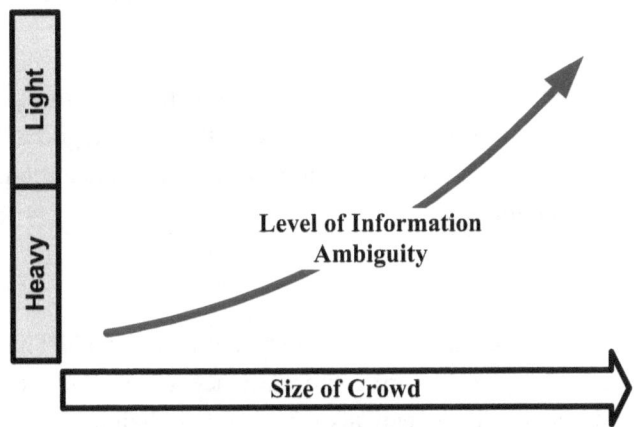

Comedy is broken down into many different components. Comedy can by employed using hyperboles, metaphors and allegories. It can also be employed by reframing topics. The subject is so large and as such we can only cover a few snippets.

Without a doubt, comedy is a challenge. Just to name a few areas of concern: we have to have good timing, a good understanding of surroundings, crowd insight, and appropriateness of content. For the purposes of our examples, we will try to set the stage as best we can to help provide additional "situational context" to make the examples more relevant.

Hyperbole (Overstatements)…

Hyperbole is any dialogue that exaggerates a point. It is a "figure" of speech that plays on the "literal". The purpose of hyperbole is to induce a strong reaction that is not to be taken seriously.

Setting the Stage: It is really late in the evening, and a struggling young author is trying to finish up his first book. He has to explain why his book is so late to his publisher.

"I stayed up until 1 million o'clock in the morning writing funny hyperboles so that the writing god wouldn't castrate my first born son as a punishment for my laziness."

Timing…

Comedic timing is based largely on a "comedic beat". These are pauses in dialogue that give the audience time to identify the joke and react. They can also be used to heighten suspense before delivering a punch line. Long pauses can be used to discern the underlying context of what the speaker is really thinking about.

Setting the Stage: A college visitor and his guide paused to admire the new Hemingway Hall that had been built on campus.

Visitor: "It is a pleasure to see a building named for Ernest Hemingway," he said.

Guide: "Actually, its named for Joshua Hemingway. No relation."

Visitor: "Was Joshua Hemingway a writer, also?"

Guide: "Yes, indeed….he wrote a check."

Reversal

A reversal is something that can have good affect on a crowd. It is especially useful in introductions for high powered individual trying to introduce themselves without coming off as too self congratulatory.

> "I would like to introduce a person that has a lot of charm, personality and charisma….unfortunately; he could not be here today…so I will try to fill in for him."

The Lighter Conclusion…

Beyond some of the basic tips found here, we should take a look out on the internet to see what else we can leverage in this area.[16] There are so many ways to make people laugh. If we are unsure about being able to deliver, try this exercise. We know ahead of time that we are going to have a couple meetings tomorrow, get online and research for a few minutes how to pull off two well timed jokes that are relevant to the topic at those meetings. Try this a couple times a week. Eventually we will have a comedic rhythm. Experimentation is good, but be careful. A couple "comedic devices" throughout the day is very helpful in any professional environment, but like medication, we can certainly over do it.

---

[16] Keyword Internet Search: "Learn Standup Comedy" or "Comedic Devices"

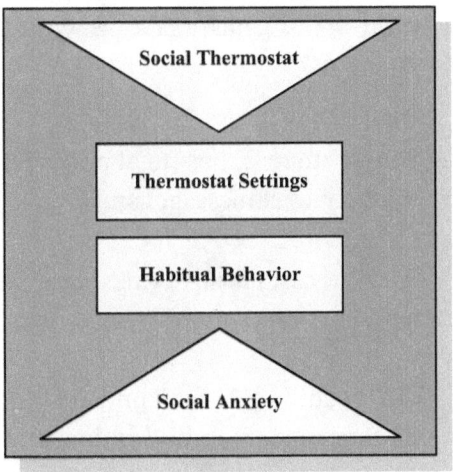

Chapter Six – Our Social Thermostat...

Big business is made when it comes to measuring personalities. Especially when we talk about how we communicate and interact with others in the work place. More and more, businesses are investing in personality/temperament testing on their employees in an effort to boost social efficiency among the work force. However, we are looking at this from a different perspective. Instead of being "labeled" through all manner of testing, it should be understood that we are approaching this from a different perspective. We should instead view ourselves as an amalgam of a single "social thermostat" that has varying ranges given a specific set of circumstances.

To understand where we are coming from we need to take a quick look at our history. We have largely classified our psyche according to three moving parts: the emotional, rational and ideal. All of our physiological brain structures are right where we left them. However, for our purposes we are more concerned about categorizing our thought process in a more palatable way for the non-scientist in the crowd.

History…

- 300 BCE – Aristotle: Ethos (total message, credibility), Pathos (an emotional message) and Logos (a logical message)[17]
- 1200 CE – Aveross: nutritive (must feed, needy), perceptive (senses and motivation), rational (logical self aware)[18]
- 1900 CE – Freud: Id (pleasure principal), Ego (reality principle), Superego (morality/cultural principle)[19]
- Present Day – Cognitive Behavioral Therapy (CBT): Emotional, Logical, Normative.[20]

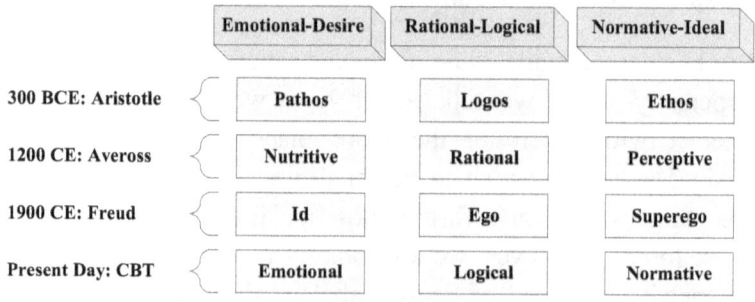

	Emotional-Desire	Rational-Logical	Normative-Ideal
300 BCE: Aristotle	Pathos	Logos	Ethos
1200 CE: Aveross	Nutritive	Rational	Perceptive
1900 CE: Freud	Id	Ego	Superego
Present Day: CBT	Emotional	Logical	Normative

More recently, over the past 20 years there has been an explosion of different behavioral analysis models. From cognitive behavioral therapy to dialectical behavior therapy, the amount of information out there is endless. For our purposes, we are not going to break down the pros and cons of each theory

---

[17] Keyword Internet Search: "Aristotle" + "Modes of Persuasion"
[18] Keyword Internet Search: "Averroes" + "Prime Matter"
[19] Keyword Internet Search: "Id, Ego and Super-Ego"
[20] Keyword Internet Search: "Cognitive Behavioral Therapy" + "Normative"

in each discipline. They are not easily understood in a single pass. They are meant to be digested by professionals who help "lead" us from point-to-point through a series of behavior modification processes.

To a large extent this is over simplifying the reality of our psyche. However, for the purposes of our discussion, we need something that is less complex, yet at the same time not so simplified, because in either case we end up with a tool that we cannot leverage. At the end of the day we do need to aggregate our thinking and come up with a way to visually represent our day-to-day thought patterns. First, we need to apply what we have learned in earlier chapters. Second, we also need to maintain a certain degree of control over the way we visually represent our professional as well as our personal dialogue. Organizing our thought patterns into a kind of "social trinity" is very helpful for a number of reasons. It can help to isolate our "goal setting" in terms of our emotions, logic and normative views. It is also helpful to see which part of our personality is in demand when discussing our "needs" versus our "wants". For starters, we want to visualize the social thermostat based on our groupings from above.

Our Social Thermostat

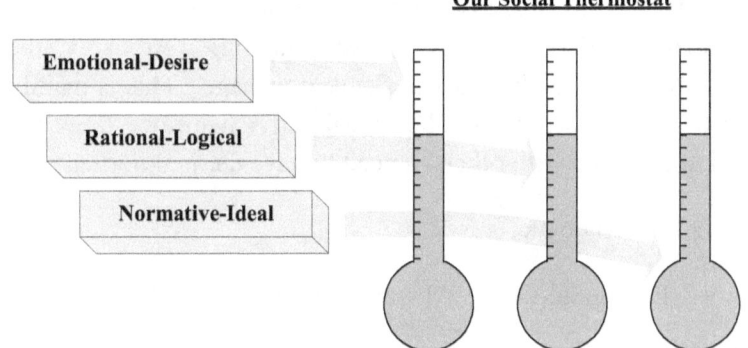

In many instances, we grossly oversimplify our personalities by labeling ourselves either introverted or extroverted. At best this is a large misrepresentation. This is not an appropriate way to view our personalities. To best apply what we have read up to this point we have to view the social thermostat from a couple different personality perspectives. We have to visually represent the social thermostat in the same way we would manage our home air conditioning thermostat. It changes all the time to meet the challenges of the elements that surround it. Our social thermostat is no different. It is a dynamic mechanism that shifts to meet the demands placed on it as it moves throughout different social surroundings.

Let us take a moment to define the three different areas of our social thermostat. The first is our "Emotional-Desire". This talks about the person inside our head that deals with our "wants". Our "wants" can be anything from that new pair of boots we have always wanted to a new person in our lives. The second area is called the "Rational-Logic". This part of our psyche is focused on quantitatively measuring our surroundings. It is occupied with rational decisions and facts. Lastly, we have the "Normative-Ideal". This portion of our psyche is qualitatively focused on integrating our surroundings. The Normative-Ideal is focused on information that is subjective, informal and descriptive of our surroundings. Arguably, the Normative-Ideal is the most difficult to manage. This is mainly due to the subjectivity of the "ideal self"…what we think we need to integrate with others, a need to have cultural normalcy.

Example in Dialogue:

- Emotional-Desire: "I want boots that are in fashion."

- Rational-Logic: "I have a pair of cool boots already. Do I really need another pair of boots? Maybe I should wait…"
- Normative-Ideal: "However, everyone else is wearing the maroon color this season…my boots are brown and out of season. This new style will help me blend."

To a large extent we instinctually adjust our social thermostat to meet certain demands (i.e. we talk differently to our parents versus our friends). Pathologies can develop when we overemphasize a portion of our social thermostat. For example, if we let our Emotional-Desire take over then we might find ourselves doing things like over spending, over/under eating, drug/alcohol abuse, or chronic gambling. If our Rational-Logic was constantly taking over, we might find ourselves constantly striving to be a perfectionist or the neighborhood "know it all".

In these cases, we succumb to a portion of our psych. We fail to recognize the power that we have inside of ourselves….that is to be deliberate and measured. While we do not realize it, most of us have an ability to purposely adjust our social thermostats. Let us take a look at a few examples of how our social thermostat can be applied to help regulate the way we interact with people.

Empathizer (Listener)

Empathizer

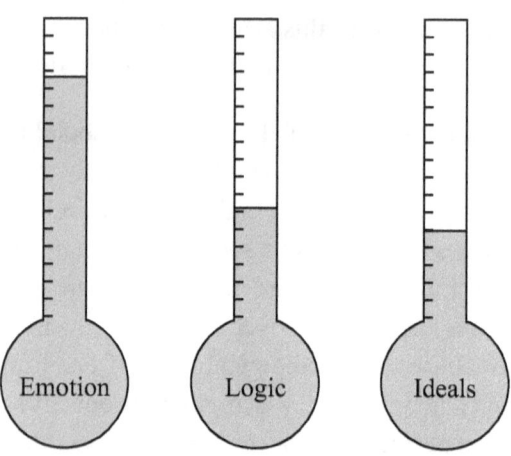

This social thermostat should be used when we are looking to be extremely open to ideas. The empathizer is the least judgmental of the thermostats. This thermostat could also be characterized as the "listening" thermostat. The idea is to be less influenced by outside norms, pressures, and rational thinking (logic). While this is a useful setting, we do not want to spend all of our time dialed in on the empathizer. For example, when tough decisions are required we need to be comfortable with dialing in the collaborator or commander settings.

Collaborator (Diplomat)

<u>Collaborator (Diplomat)</u>

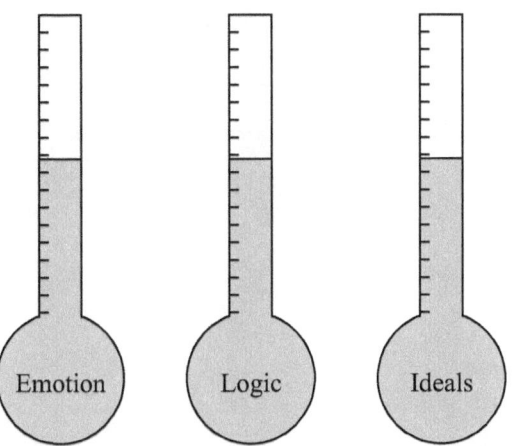

The collaborator is the balanced thermostat. We are using all areas in concert and can understand many different perspectives with a good balance of emotion, ideals and logic. This thermostat is very helpful, and a place that many should strive to find throughout the day. There is a downside to being the diplomat in that we can sometimes be viewed as "riding the fence". While we want to develop a collaborative thermostat, we should learn to switch on the commander and empathizer as needed given the situation.

Commander (Field Marshal)

Commander

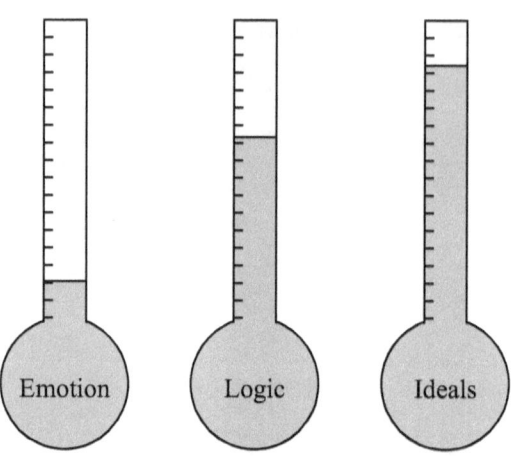

The commander personality is high on ideals. This person can be seen as a bit of a perfectionist. While still logical, this social thermostat is best used in situations where executive decisions need to be made quickly and without emotions. Commanders can be "single step" or "evolutionary" minded in execution. Single step commanders think very linearly. In other words, they must have a complete roadmap and must complete it in stepwise fashion. An evolutionary commander is comfortable with leaping into the unknown. While this setting is helpful in the absence of organization, we do not want to be fixated on the command temperature all the time. Running around barking orders all day long can get old and exhausting.

Splitter (Polarizer, Black-n-White)

Splitter

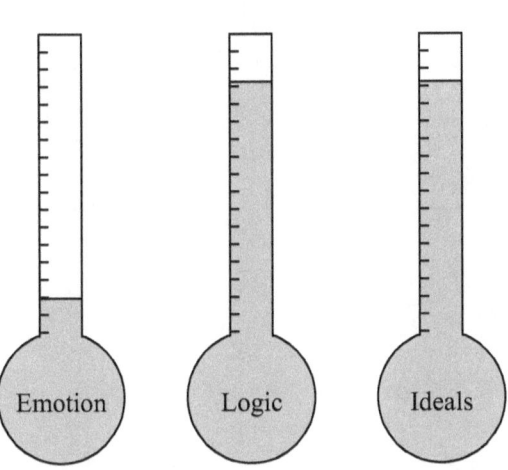

The splitter is similar to a narcissist. The main difference is that a splitter uses logic to split ideas up into compartmentalized camps. There is no grey area in this line of thinking. It is either this or that…no in between…no other solution. This is a social thermostat that does not contain much value. It is mainly illustrated here to show that if we find ourselves in this situation that we should find a way to dial down both our logic and ideals and dial up some emotions. We want to get the splitter thermostat down to a "realist" perspective, which is less abrasive. Lastly, this thermostat setting turns off our alternative analysis thinking and can get us stuck in execution loops. Put another way, this mode set in a chronic state ensures that we continue to make polarizing decisions as we move throughout our social settings.

Idealist (the normative points of view)

Idealist

The idealist is high on ideals and mediocre on emotions. We exhibit this behavior when we are lacking in factual evidence. When we cannot appeal to logic, we instinctually try to appeal to emotional or social norms. This thermostat is helpful in strategic lofty discussions not bound by logic. Interesting enough, the idealist thermostat will not get us in trouble inside the academic community (many of the professors are idealist and romantics to begin with), the place this will get us in trouble is in operational settings (like military, police, etc…). The world of idealist does not bode well in these circles.

Romantic (similar to Idealist, but with more emotions)

Romantic

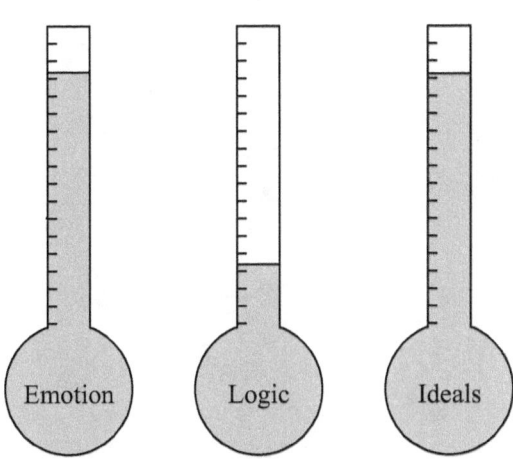

The romantic thermostat is similar to the idealist thermostat. A romantic thermostat usually tosses out logic all together. Romantics are utopian visionaries. It is when ideals are paired with strong emotions, such as love or fear. A romantic social thermostat setting is not necessarily bad. It is good to have lofty ideals backed by strong emotions, but it can sometimes lead to very uncompromising attitudes. A true romantic will overlook pragmatics.

Realist (Pragmatist)

Realist (Pragmatist)

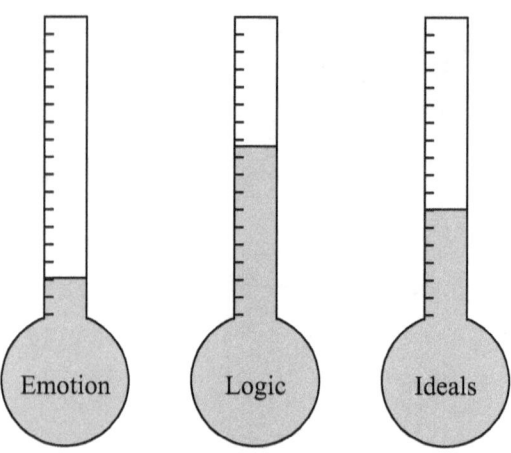

A realist social thermostat setting does not deal in emotional states very well. A realist values what is occurring as of this very moment. This is an "it is what it is" mentality. This is very useful in operational settings. We do not want to get stuck on this thermostat for extremely long periods of time. A chronic reality setting on our thermostat can get a person stuck in non-creative, status quo thinking. Where a romantic will push the boundaries of reality, a realist will stay within the boundaries of reality.

Narcissist (the know-it-all, bragger, etc…)

Narcissist (aka know-it-all)

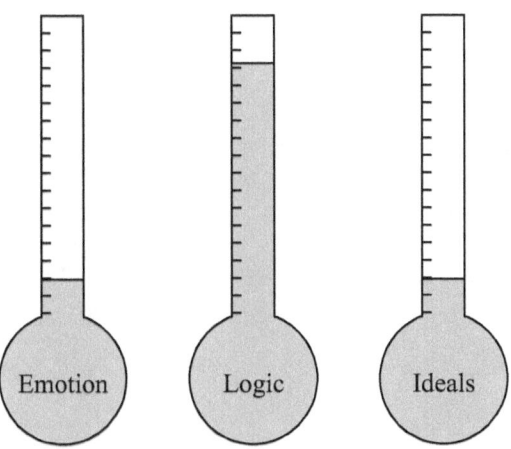

Let's face it; we are all a little narcissistic. From the moment we are born, we are needy folks. So it is helpful to clarify what we are defining as narcissist. Narcissism in this context is a person that is high on logic, and low on emotional apathy, or social norms (ideals). Logic is used ad nauseam to discredit any and all who are willing to listen. In addition, the know-it-all thermostat will get us in trouble when we least expect it. This is a setting that should largely be avoided all together. The problem with this setting is that all appeals for information and personal confirmation are rooted in what we think we know. At its core this is a personality trait that is based on keeping up with the Jones'. A chronic narcissistic attitude will have us always basing our self-worth on artificial measures (i.e. how much we think we know, the number of online friends, size of our contact lists, or the size of our new house).

Sleeper (...in the literal sense...)

Sleeper

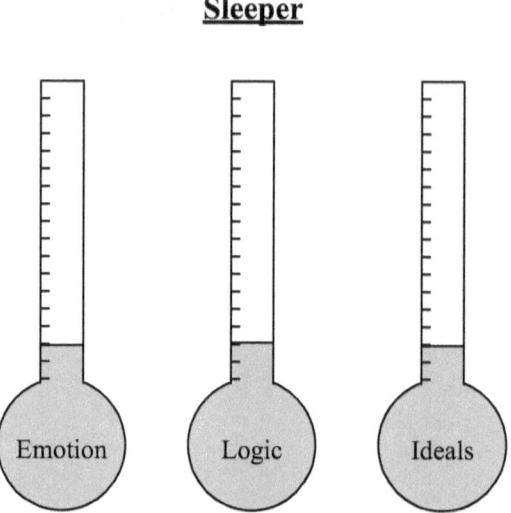

Get some sleep, as it is good to dial everything down every once and a while. Meditative states are also applicable here as well. Dialing all of these different settings down helps to reset and reengage. This is especially true when we find that our thermostat gets out of range.

Wrapping up the Social Thermostat...

The key to mastering this concept starts with observation. Much of our ability to observe ourselves is biased. That is why we need to integrate both what we recognize in ourselves, and evaluate that against what other see in us. Often times, the two views do not line up. There is what we think we are...then there is what people see. That is why it is critical to be an open individual that is accepting of change. Our ritual behavior can be very difficult to break, it can also lead to chronic social pathologies that we are not cognizant of. Let us take a moment to review how our social thermostat can help us in these areas.

Our Social Thermostat and Ritual Behavior…

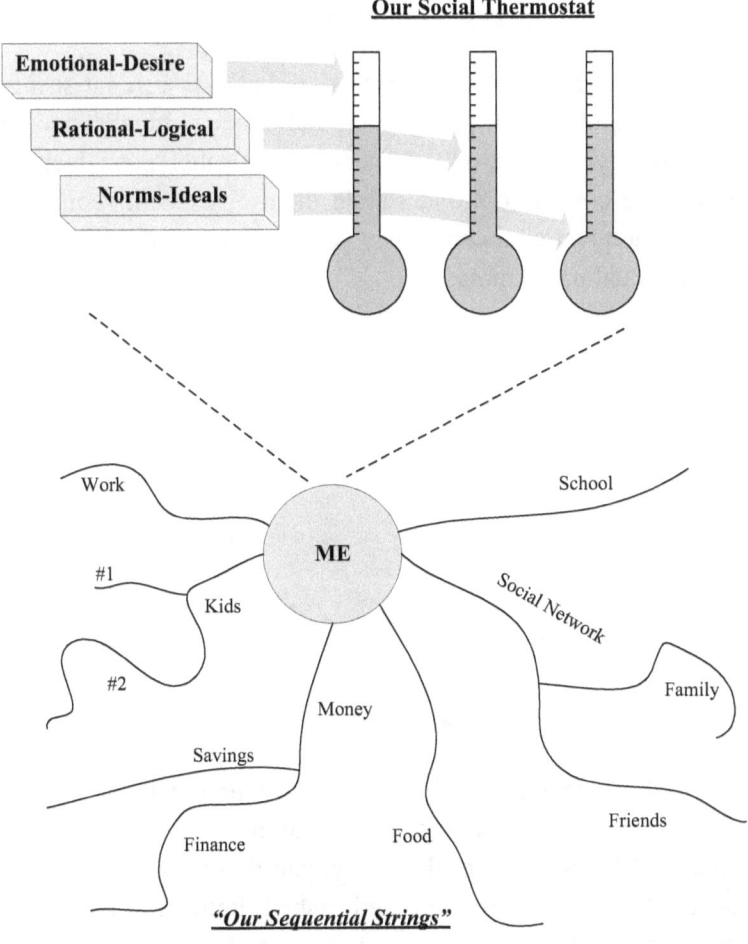

Non-scientifically speaking, we like to sequence our lives in task oriented ways. These behavioral strings are like linear work streams in our daily routine. For many of us, this is especially clear to people who are raising kids. We get up, we take a shower, we brush our teeth, we put on our clothes, we get the kids ready for school, we drop the kids off at school, we go to work and start the remainder of our day which will have multiple strings as well. This is really important because to a certain extent this makes or breaks individuals.

Some people innately carry scissors so that they can cut strings at certain points in a sequence such that they can break behavior more quickly than others. Others on the other hand lack an appropriate cutting tool and saddle themselves with sequential strings that never go away....they get tangled up and begin to tie the individual up in knots.

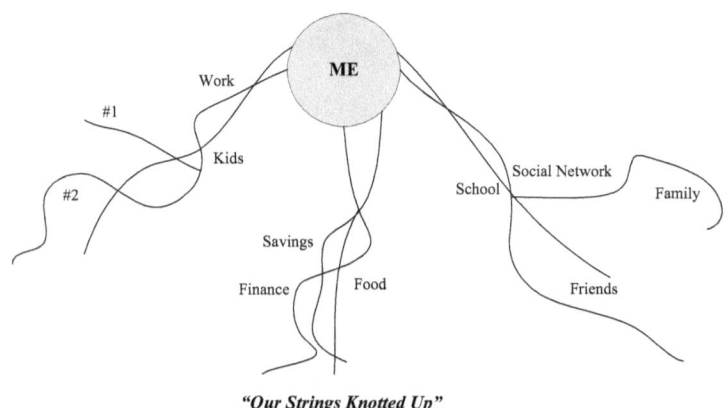

"Our Strings Knotted Up"

We need to understand that our ability to create behavioral strings is rooted in our "habitual" nature. It is through our procedural learning style, that we create these sequences. It is also used to deeply program, and embed, items into our social framework so that we do them with very little thought. This ritualistic behavior is not all bad; after all it keeps us on task. Rituals are easier to execute because they decrease the amount of variability that we have to keep track of in our daily routines.

On the other hand, we can get ourselves in trouble if we do not periodically review our ritualistic behavior. This can be problematic because our daily work streams can get tangled up when we take on too much throughout our lives. This can lead to social pressures, anxieties and depression. Persistent issues can manifest themselves physically through anxiety, pressure, depression or mania. And in many cases these persistent issues can lead to unmanageable situations. Which is truly a sad state to live in all the time, anyone who has experienced severe anxiety, or depression, understands that it truly is a mind killer. For many, we experience anxiety in small acute cases that are separated by a fair amount of time throughout our lives. (e.g. death of a significant other, lose of employment, speaking on stage, etc…). However, for some this is a routine, debilitating curse that can rob people from enjoying even the smallest events in their lives.

Conclusion…

Even the most simple of strings will elude us, to a certain extent we have to be in a state of mind that allows us the opportunity to be wrong. We also need to recognize a need for change. Once we have accepted failure and change as being okay, we can then begin the process of being honest with ourselves. Thus we can more clearly elucidate what it is that needs to be corrected in our lives. However, for many of us, we for all of our processing power are unable to untangle the mess that we sometimes create. Social anxiety can set in to create a truly sticky situation. No amount of self introspection will uncover the complexities of our social strings. In these cases, it is best advised to get outside help. Remember that there is what we think we are and then there is what people see. We often need outside guidance to reconcile the two views. This can be in the form of clinical counseling, peer review, or work performance evaluation. Above all else, we have to be open to change to make a difference. Status quo is easy, change is hard, but change is the color of life that we need not miss.

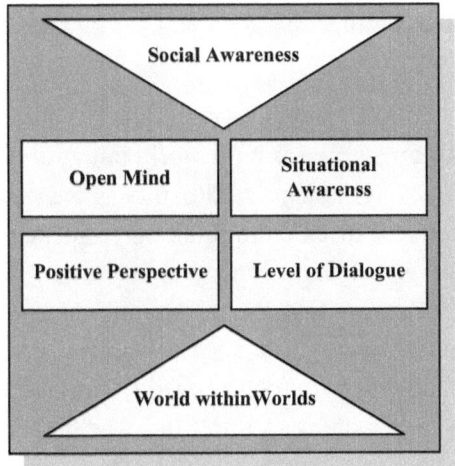

Chapter Seven – It's All About Perspective...

Social awareness is defined as an awareness of other social groups and communities. [21] It is an awareness of the behavior, culture and difficulties that each of the other social groups face. But we should take this a step further. For us this is not just awareness, this is ownership. We do not want to simply "see" the other community; we need to also "be" the other community

Our social awareness has a lot to do with how successful we cultivate and maintain our personal and professional relationships. So it is important for us to develop a longitudinal awareness of our social surroundings. In developing an ability to visually represent social interactions, we also increase our overall awareness. There are five primary components that inform our awareness: having an open mind, maintaining a positive perspective, understanding events and actions

---

[21]Keyword Internet Search: "Social Awareness" + "Emotional Intelligence"

(situations), understanding the level of dialogue, and seeing our movement through other social domains.

Open Mind…

Maintaining an open mind is hard work, but gets easier the more we practice it. A status quo community is easy to sign up for, hence why so many of us end up taking residence here at some point in our lives. Like so many mind killers, close minded thinking is a behavior that has to be mitigated. Going about opening up one's mind is a very rewarding process. It can expose us to new ideas, foods, music, cultures and ways of thinking. Open mindedness turns the world around us into a treasure; it allows us to appreciate the variety and intricacies of life. Furthermore, an open mind increases our social awareness. So keep the following in mind when navigating the social landscape:

- Maintain a world view by learning from different people and lifestyles.
    o For Example:
        - Actually learn about what Marxism really means instead of hearing it second hand from a politician.
        - Spend some time with an underrepresented community that we are completely unfamiliar with.
- Learn from atypical, odd or strange sources. In other words, beware of mob mentality…take the road less traveled.
    o For Example:
        - Take an introductory course at a local community college in anthropology,

    human trafficking or eastern European folk lore.

- Research strange or fascinating topics online.
- Introduce ourselves to a new language.

- Learn a new physical skill. The idea is to get out of our comfort zones.
  - For Example:
    - Take dance, karate or skiing classes.
    - Learn something completely unusual or new like hang gliding or snowboarding.
- Exercise the political mind.
  - For Example:
    - Take a hot topic political issue and learn both sides of the arguments.
    - Be an unbiased entity and argue both sides of a case.
- Learn to be an outsider.
  - For Example:
    - Travel to a country that puts us on the outside of a crowd. Observe our feelings and see how others who are outsiders in our home country might be feeling.
    - Always had the luxury of a car? Take public transportation for a week to see how others might struggle without something so basic.
- Spend some time with a complete stranger, or a person from an underrepresented population.
  - For Example:
    - Spend some time at an LGBT (Lesbian, Gay, Bisexual, or Transgender) support

group meeting. We will be amazed at what happens to our perspective on people when we ACTUALLY meet people in person.

- Have a casual conversation with a homeless person the next time we are out shopping for an expensive coat. It is as simple as saying, "Hi my name is…"

- Force ourselves into situations we are scared of.
  - For Example:
    - Speak up at a large gathering, or better yet, be a guest speaker at local group meetings.
    - Buy a mechanics manual for the car and replace the brake pads. We will be surprised at how easy it is, and how much money we will save.
    - Make an appointment with the CEO of the company to introduce ourselves. We will be surprised how many CEOs like to hear straight talk versus what people think they want to hear.

Positive Perspective…

It does sound cliché when someone says, "You have to maintain a positive attitude". Yet, for some reason we write it off as psycho-babble speak. We come up with creative ways to dwell on negative emotions, thoughts and behavior. Our justification for this behavior is largely grounded in what we perceive to be reality. Unfortunately, we often believe that pragmatic thinking requires us to partake in negative thinking. Nothing is further from the truth; reality is independent of the observer. Roughly translated this means that life moves on with or without us. Which means that only one thing is left, a person's approach to reality: either positive or negative. A positive pragmatic is a powerful force.

It is a tough universe that we live in. It is a place where organisms are consuming each other to survive. It is a place where humans are stripping the planet to survive. It is a place where our sun will eventually explode, destroying Earth in the process. The reality of life is harsh and it is easy to see how easily it is to get caught up in negative behavior. There are tragedies in the world, but we know that life moves on with or without us. This means that our behavior and outlook is within our control.

Here are some tips that cultivate a positive perspective:

- Negative situations have positive outcomes.
    - For Example:
        - A mistake is knowledge attained of what not to do next time.
        - Just because we failed our first physics quiz does not mean that we will fail the class.
        - Persistently failing job interviews is an intelligence gathering exercise. It lets us know what we do not know.
- Positive situations are reinforced by positive outcomes
    - For Example:
        - Success that is built on success reinforces that we are on the right path.
- A flawless person does not exist
    - For Example:

- Even the best physician will make mistakes, if we find one that says otherwise than we need to find a new medical doctor.
- Adversity is a reality; it is our responsibility to take it from there.
  - For Example:
    - Life changing events happen; it is a fact of life. However, our perspective is within our control. We can choose to dwell in the negative or the positive.
    - In sports, a good football quarterback realizes that dwelling on interceptions will result in more interceptions.
- Traditional thinking nets traditional results
  - For Example:
    - Just because everyone on the block owns a luxury sport utility vehicle, does not mean that we have to own one.
    - Money/Business models target the masses (i.e. single family homes, fast food restaurants, car dealerships, etc…)
    - Take the Scenic Route: Going to the Giza Necropolis is great if we want to fight the crowds, instead think about visiting the Valley of the Kings.

Situational Awareness…

Situational Awareness is defined as "…being aware of what is happening around you to understand how information, events, and your own actions will impact your goals and objectives, both now and in the near future."[22]

We are constantly comparing and contrasting our perceptions of reality with actual reality. We calculate our next moves based on information that we receive. Situational Awareness was first used by the United States Air Force (USAF) in the 1950s and 1960s.[23] It was determined by the USAF that survivability of air-to-air engagements was best achieved when observing the opponent and anticipating their next move based on prior moves.

Developing situational awareness takes practice and patience:

- Learn to feel and sense your surroundings.
  - o For Example:
    - During an interview for a job we notice that one of the interviewers constantly looking at their watch before the interview even starts. Probably means that they are not interested in anything we have to say. So what do we have to lose?
    - On our way to the grocery store, we wisely work the fringe of the parking lot instead of driving thru the main street directly in front of the store.
- Actively contrast your perceptions and reality.
  - o For Example:
    - We avoid the agitated boss. Yet we cannot help but feel that we are the reason for our Boss' discontent. So we

---

[22] Keyword Internet Search: "Situational Awareness"
[23] Keyword Internet Search: "Situational Awareness" + "USAF"

> compare our Boss' reaction to other employees before making our next move.
> - What we outwardly portray and what is actually received are two different things. We thought that a simple single word response in an email was sufficient due to our busy schedule, but the receiver of the email thought otherwise.

Level of Dialogue...

This is one of the more important concepts to understand. The level of dialogue should be used as a way to target our conversation. Socially speaking it is a tough world, and it is getting tougher. One of the best ways to interoperate with other people is to understand how our own dialogue is landing on others in relation to the general spoken atmosphere.

Carl von Clausewitz is a famous general of Prussian descent. A late nineteenth century strategist, he is famously attributed to the term "fog of war". It is a conceptual way to organize the natural gaps that occur in our situational awareness.[24] Clausewitzian theory and practice has been augmented since "On War" was published posthumously in 1832.

---

[24] Carl von Clausewitz was a politico-military strategist. Clausewitz illustrates famously, "The great uncertainty of all data in war is a peculiar difficulty, because all action must, to a certain extent, be planned in a mere twilight, which in addition not infrequently—like the effect of a fog or moonshine—gives to things exaggerated dimensions and unnatural appearance." -Clausewitz, Carl von, On War, Book 2, Chapter 2, Paragraph 24, 1832

"Fog of War"

- Grand Strategic
  - Social and political aspects of war
- Military Strategic
  - Structure and capability of military
- Operational
  - Analysis of strategic priorities and intelligence
- Tactical
  - Execution of strategic and operational goals

Clausewitz was focused on mitigating uncertainty and friction in grand strategies and military tactics, but he was also versed in the political machinery of statecraft. His ideas on information gaps and friction in battle easily translate to our socially constructed frameworks. From this perspective we can assemble our thoughts with a level of appropriateness when we interact with others.

Here are some examples of each level:

- Political Discourse – This type of dialogue is very generic it is focused on shaping policy.
  - "We are going to create policies and laws governing the use of information systems."
- Strategic Discourse – Strategic discourse is at the crosswords between where "work" actually occurs (tactical and operational) and where policy decisions are handed down from senior executives in the organization. This level may involve the creation of policy; however, dialogue at this level is focused on the development of roadmaps used to execute policy decisions made in higher levels.

- o "We will create regulations, standards and roadmaps for the information system project plan."
- Operational Discourse – This is where conversations translate strategic dialogue into actionable work items (task tracking, work items, deliverables, timelines, etc...). After strategy has been crafted, tactical plans are drawn up to determine the actual implementation or management of a project, system or line of work.
    - o "We will create a project plan and schedule for the deployment of the information system."
- Tactical Discourse – Conversations at this level are based on day-to-day work items. It is focused on schedules, product development or production, etc...
    - o "We are developing and creating the information system."

<u>Level of Dialogue:</u>

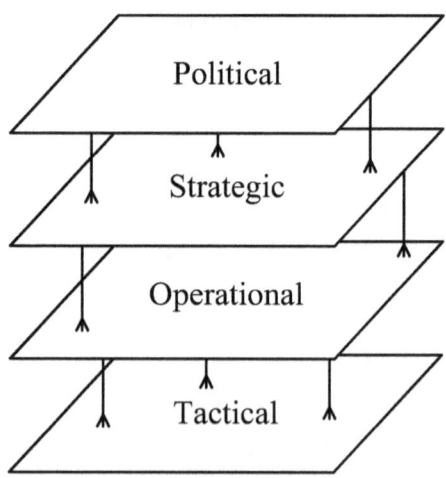

The level of dialogue determines the context of the interaction. In summary, we need to have a good handle on the environment that we are navigating. When we move through our social circles we need to keep our overall social awareness focused on maintaining an open mind, a positive perspective, situational awareness and a level of dialogue. If in the process of our day-to-day activities, we can keep this moving forward as a working visual representation in our social interactions with others, our ability to interoperate and connect with other people will significantly increase.

World within Worlds…

Lastly, for us to fully appreciate our social surroundings we need to have a "world within worlds" framework in mind when we are moving through our daily interactions with people. While the "level of dialogue" is a "vertical" view of discourse, the "world within worlds" perspective can be seen as a "horizontal" view of discourse.

For example, an employee is talking to their boss. In this conversation, the boss is trying to better understand the complexities of the employee's work for the day. During the course of this conversation the boss makes a joke about Asian work ethics, not realizing that the employee is half Asian.

This does not strictly apply to our ancestry, but it also applies to our background in other parts of our lives. We are all in different worlds throughout our lives. Some of us are church leaders while being a janitor at a local elementary school. Some of us are a combination of football coaches, attorneys and National Guard members. The point is that we all have different hats we wear throughout our daily lives that put us in different social networks. We have to be cognizant as best we can to understand these different worlds we run thru.

Chapter Seven Summary…

All of these topics taken together combine to form our social awareness. When we move through our various social circles we need to keep in mind all these different aspects. We will not be mistake free, but this will certainly help us move towards a better process in our communication ability.

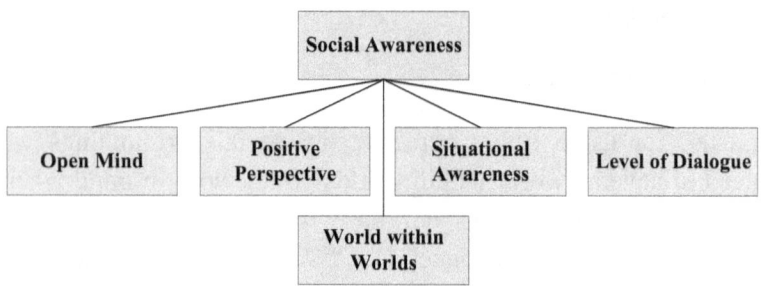

The next time we approach our friends, colleagues, social groups or family members it is a good idea to keep the following in mind:

I.   First, keep an open mind, do not approach a social interaction with preconceived ideas

II.   Second, maintain a positive and upbeat demeanor and perspective

III.   Third, be mindful of the non-verbal environment

     a.   Their body language (hunched, puffed out, arms crossed, leaning in, fiddling with keys, etc…)

     b.   Identifying information (medical bracelets, jewelry, college mascots, etc…)

     c.   Understand the physical placement of the discussion (public, private, closed door, elevator, water cooler, etc…)

IV.   Fourth, we want to understand the level at which social interactions are occurring (political, strategic, tactical or operational), so be inquisitive.

V.   Lastly, we want to keep the "world within worlds" social framework in mind.

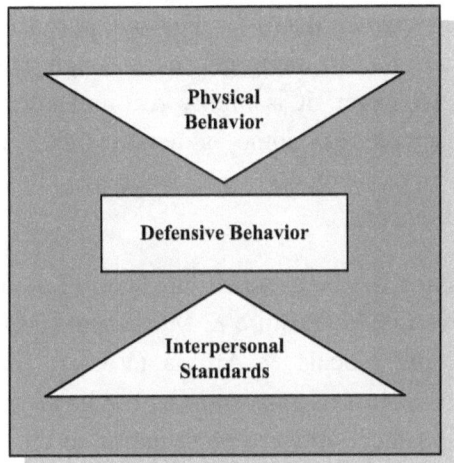

Chapter Eight – Physical & Defensive Behavior...

There are many ways that we reveal ourselves to the world. First, we need to be very aware of our physical body language. Our body language says so much about what is on our mind. Second, we need to spend some time focused on how defensive behavior impacts not only our inner dialogue but also how we are viewed externally by others. Lastly, we will talk about personal standards; we can sometimes be our own worst critic, yet we underutilize our ability to be our own most amazing advocate.

Physical Behavior...

Our physical behavior says so much about our character. From our hair styles to our body posture, we communicate with the outside world constantly. It goes without saying; our physical behavior has a direct effect on every encounter we come across with other people. When we talk about physical behavior we are concerned about the audio, visual and chemical.

There are numerous self-help web sites and books that address these issues in greater detail[25]. For our purposes we need a quick reference list to help get us through the day-to-day interactions. However, it is highly recommended to do some additional research as some situations call for different "physicalities and protocols" (i.e. weddings, board meetings, military functions, etc...).

Physical behavior can be grouped into the following categories: Dress & Attire (D&A), Posture & Movement (P&M), Hands & Face (H&F), and Vocals & Aroma (V&A). Each of these particular areas is just as important as the next. Together they represent our physical outward presentation to the world. D&A covers a range of items: hair, nails, clothing, and shoes. P&M describes how we physically carry ourselves while sitting or walking. H&F covers the movement of our hands and our facial expressions. V&A being the non-visual senses (i.e. auditory and olfactory) describes the volume and style of our speech pattern.

✓ Dress & Attire
  o Unkempt head hair, crazy facial hair, unclean nails, inappropriate clothes – Comedy club here we come! Did my friends leave me in a dark alley over night?
  o Clean cut head and facial hair, clean nails, appropriate to the occasion clothing – The board meeting is about to begin. I am ready for battle.
  o Formal Wear – This means we are serious and intend to make a statement, or speech...or we just want to look good for no reason.

---

[25] Keyword Internet Search: "Body Language" + "Nonverbal Communication"

- o Business Wear – I have three thousand meetings compressed into a mere eight hours. Did you want something?
- o Informal Wear – Martini is a new friend I found down at the bar.
- o House Wear – Research shows that gravitational fields increase the closer you get to home. My shirts are just so damn heavy!
- o Underarm Stains – Bad….we cannot say anything more about this topic.

✓ Posture & Movement
- o Hunched – It means we are not engaged, sheepish or timid.
- o Puffy Chest – This means we are confident and engaged.
- o Walking Slowly – It may indicate to others that we are not busy or not engaged.
- o Walking Fast – It means we are on a mission and with purpose.
- o Walking with a Bounce – May indicate that we are positive and jubilant.

✓ Hands & Face
- o Hands Facing Up – This may indicate that we are receptive and open
- o Hands Facing Down – This may signal that we are not open to new ideas or we may be defensive.
- o Clenched Fists – This may also suggest that we are not receptive to new ideas or adversarial.
- o Arms Crossed – This is the universal defensive signal.
- o Hiding Hands (in pockets, behind back) – May indicate that we are not telling a complete story…we are looking to hide something.

- o Fast Moving Arms – Emphatic behavior...it makes us appear like a crazy salesman.
- o General fidgeting and erratic movements – This indicates that we are either not ready for battle or we are extremely nervous.
- o Looking Up – This means that we are in visualization mode and are trying to really concentrate and tune out others.
- o Looking Down – This is a look of submission. It means we are looking for support.
- o Raising, or Furrowing, Eyebrows – A fairly commonly understood motion, it means we are questioning the information.
- o Leaning In or Head Tilting – Means we are interested in the conversation. It says we are inquisitive and sends a message that we are listening.
- o Leaning Back – We are disengaged and not interested in the task or topic at hand.
- o Pursing our Lips – We are angry.
- o Nose Scratching – Might indicate that we are not being truthful about information...or it might indicate that we just have an itchy nose.
- o Smirk – This indicates that we are not impressed, we are not interested in the information or topic being discussed.
- o Full Smile – A full smile involves our eyes as well. It indicates that we are happy, engaged and approving.
- ✓ Vocals & Aroma
  - o High Volume – No not yelling, but a command voice is indicative of confidence. It sends a message that we know our information well.

- o Low Volume – A low volume indicates that we are unsure of ourselves. It sends a message that we are timid.
- o Erratic Volume – This means that our confidence in the topic at hand is flimsy. At times we understand the information, other times we are lost.
- o Bad Breath – Not inviting...just bad...really bad.
- o Fresh Breath – Nice and clean...inviting. Fresh is good.
- o Bad Body Smell – The workout smell is not in fashion. It indicates that we are supremely rushed, or just got out of a gym.
- o Fragrant Body Smell – If we create more bodily odor than normal consider using a stronger perfume (Eau de Perfume). However, for most of us we can stick with the regular stuff (Eau de Toilette or Eau de Cologne).

It needs to be understood that this is a two way street. We need to keep this list in mind with our own behavior, but we can also use this list to recognize behavior in others. For example, it is helpful to know when people begin to lean back, or rattle their keys in a conversation. Understanding the basics of nonverbal communication can go a long way to help make social interactions more successful.

Defensive Behavior...

Defensive behavior is very dangerous. We have all been put into positions that we felt required us to engage in defensive behavior. Defensive behavior is the quickest route to losing credibility...even when we believe we are right.

Our ideas and behavior need to be open to interpretation. When we subject our behavior to criticism we are accepting that we do not know everything and being honest with ourselves is the only way that we grow in this respect. Defensive behavior causes us to lose not only outward public credibility, but it inhibits our internal growth. It closes us off to the world. When we instead open our ideas and behavior up, we are showing that we are thinking of a bigger picture and are more accepting of different points of view.

Our Interpersonal Standards...

From adversaries to advocates, often times we look at these two areas as being separated (i.e. we have our personal life and we have our professional life, never will the two meet). However, we do not want to overlook how our social dynamics interrelate with each other and affect both worlds. Being surrounded by "friends" does not necessarily mean that we still are not being "interviewed". Our friends judge and measure us based on their own internal biases. Our family members (as probably the worst offenders of this phenomenon) are constantly putting us in the proverbial "fish bowl". So when we talk about "the interview", we are really talking about any interaction that is meant to "size" up another individual so that they can be compared against a standard.

The standards come in many forms. They can be a personal opinion, qualification, certification, ideological or philosophical. In the end we are compared against "standards" all throughout our lives. With that said, some will philosophically view themselves as being a person that is a non-conformist, or non-standards based. In other words, "I will be the judge of what is best for me." However, it is faulty from two perspectives. First, whether we like it or not we are all held to a standard (e.g. that of others or that of our own). Second, if we hold ourselves based on a standard of our own design then we are truly doing ourselves a disservice by not allowing our standards to be open to interpretation. In a way, our own standards that we create for ourselves are inherently flawed.

Our preconceived standards are designed to conform to our own level of comfort with the world around us (we all have biases that we bring to the table). We do not grow if we do not open up our mind to a different way of thinking. It is only through social challenges that we grow. We can challenge our standards by subjecting them to scrutiny. We approach this process with open arms. We become agents of change and openness. A strong mind is an open mind. The more we subject our internal standards to criticism the more we strengthen our own thought process.

.

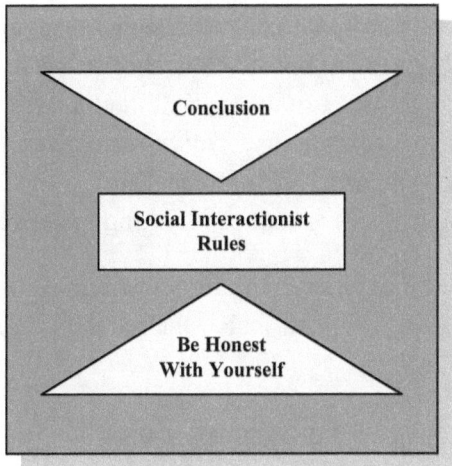

Chapter Nine – Conclusion

If we have gotten this far then we are on our way to seeing the world around us in more vivid color and detail. When we interact with people, groups, friends and family members we go thru our mental rolodex in a rather pre-conditioned manner. If there is any single take away from this process then it should be that we want to condition ourselves to be more deliberate and measured in our social interactions.

We want to push the envelope; we want to try new and different things we want to be open to other ideas and communities of interest. We are not saying that one should be a constant "yes person" but we are saying that for a person to be successful they should be available to the moment. In other words, go to a local conference, speak to people we would not normally, take a class that pushes our limit, and always try to "own"...died in the wool...no holds barred...own the moment. If there is anything that is overlooked more in life...it is ownership. We are not talking about owning a car, house or materials items. These materials are here today and gone tomorrow. Instead, we are talking about our personal moments, endeavors and goals. We have to be willing to put ourselves in another person's shoes and own that view, get comfortable with it, understand "the why" of that personality or community. Only then will we be able to see that the world is so much richer than "Me" and "You", or "Us" against the "World"...it is about everything in between.

Here are some rules to keep in mind when going about our day-to-day activities. We call them the "Visual Social Interactionist" rules:

The "Visual Social Interactionist" Rules:

- o Do not be afraid of change
- o Keep an open mind
- o Actively exercise our "social awareness"
- o Maintain temporal perspective
- o Have three alternate plans
- o Practice our visual interactions daily
- o Be deliberate and mindful of our social surroundings
- o Be honest with, and able to laugh, at ourselves
- o The glass IS always "half full"

We need to keep in mind that while we learn new perspectives and new ways of thinking we have to revisit old ideas and incorporate new ideas. Lastly, we want to be honest with ourselves throughout the process. We are all human and often mislead ourselves; at the very least we need to work towards being honest with ourselves. It is a socially tough world out there, utterly brutal. Self-honesty is the starting point in seeing the world around us. We cannot always win the self-honesty battle. We have to tell ourselves that it is okay to "fail"...we break down and make mistakes ALL the time. Yet, admitting failure is a HUGE success story in and of itself. In reality, we are really good at seeing only what we want to see. How can we grow if we do not first admit that we fail? The truth is we do not grow; we stagnate in the "status quo". We need to have a healthy dose of humor and perspective. When we make mistakes, we have to laugh at them and move on.

Admitting that we fail is the beginning of success.

Acknowledgments:

I would like to thank my wife and kids in supporting me in this endeavor. I would like to especially thank my wife for taking time out of her life to help me understand what the balance of life really means. Lastly, I cannot forget my parents. Where others were closed to variety and change, they afforded me an opportunity to navigate life with choices, options and an open mind.

About the Author:

Growing up as a soft spoken kid, I was always impressed with other people's ability to talk. On standardized testing, I excelled at the more mechanical and visual-spatial sections. I was never really good at getting what was in my head out into spoken language. My first real computer job was working at a small local computer store fixing personal computers. I had a knack for the technical. Shortly after high school, and with no college, I was hired to look after an IBM mainframe on the night shift at a health maintenance organization. I loved it; I was largely left alone to manage the backups, job queues and nightly requests. As I moved through my information technology career, I learned a few programming languages, became a database administrator and would eventually end up being a systems architect at a "Big 4" consulting firm. And I have to say it has been very rewarding. I started out in IT when consulting was good and people overlooked my quirky, introverted demeanor. Before settling down at a formal consulting firm, my background allowed me to work as an independent "street" consultant for 24 different companies over the course of 16 years.

As I reflect back, I wondered what I did to get where I am today. My performance in high school did not paint a pretty picture. Running through the South Dade Florida scene during the 80s and 90s was not helpful. It was truly the "wild wild south". I was headed for disaster and it was not pretty. I graduated high school by the width of a hair. I was completely unprepared for college, or the professional work force for that matter. I enrolled in college, but quickly dropped out. What saved me was that I had a knack for picking up computer languages. Unfortunately, I was a little too self congratulatory in my early years. Fortunately, I was in for a comprehensive attitude adjustment.

My wife gave me one of the biggest gifts ever, the gift of perspective. We had our normal course of arguments. And like any "normal person" I initially thought that these arguments were bad. Luckily I learned to embrace these discussions. First, my wife was able to open me up to new ideas and ways of thinking. Second, she was able to slowly breakdown my deeply rooted biases. Lastly, she got me back to college. All together, this was huge for me. Next to my children, they became the greatest eye openers of my life.

I learned that success in our personal and professional life does not come from brute "raw intelligence" or never ending "hard work". While this certainly does not hurt, I started to see that collaboration, openness to new ideas, broad spectrum perspectives and healthy doses of optimistic behavior relate more to how successful a person becomes in their personal and professional endeavors. Social literacy is a critical factor to success and I had to become an expert in this field, or perish personally and professionally. Social literacy has both a transformative and cascading affect on our lives. Our greatest achievements are largely grounded in our development of tools that can be applied in our everyday social settings. For some, social mechanics and group dynamics come easy. Some are born with an innate ability to work a crowd, while others struggle to get the gist of a basic smile. During the second half of my career I became fascinated with how seasoned socialites could "cold read" a crowd, or how a manager could leverage non-verbal queues in tough conversations. Thus, I started to approach social situations from a completely different angle. Since my brain was not built like other more seasoned socialites, I instead began to leverage my stronger ability to visualize data structures and information flow (i.e. the complex and abstract). In other words, I started to develop a simplified visual process to help me represent my dialogue.

I also realized the difficulty we all have in relaying information to each other. This is especially exacerbated by our newfound social media technologies. I found that our ability to interoperate with each other was not just a business problem, but a systemic problem that permeates every aspect of our lives. So instead of getting my degree in a technical discipline I switched majors my senior year and got my degree in anthropology from the University of Kansas. As such, I consider myself an "anthro-tech" person of sorts and going forward I will always be on the lookout for ways to bridge the social as well as the technical.

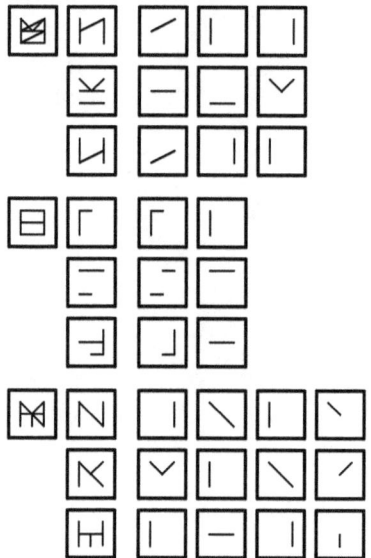

Index:

www.ingramcontent.com/pod-product-compliance
Lightning Source LLC
Chambersburg PA
CBHW051428280526
45785CB00003B/1208